At-Risk Students Defy the Odds

Overcoming Barriers to Educational Success

Rosa Aronson

scarecrow education

The Scarecrow Press, Inc.
A Scarecrow Education Book
Lanham, Maryland, and London
2001

SCARECROW PRESS, INC.
A Scarecrow Education Book

Published in the United States of America
by Scarecrow Press, Inc.
4720 Boston Way, Lanham, Maryland 20706
www.scarecroweducation.com

4 Pleydell Gardens, Folkestone
Kent CT20 2DN, England

British Library Cataloguing in Publication Information Available

Library of Congress Cataloging-in-Publication Data

Aronson, Rosa, 1953-
At-risk students defy the odds : overcoming barriers to educational success / Rosa Aronson.
p. cm. — (A Scarecrow education book)
Includes bibliographical references.
ISBN 0-8108-3992-X (alk. paper) — ISBN 0-8108-3993-8 (pbk. : alk. paper)
1. Socially handicapped children—Education—United States—Case studies. 2. Academic achievement—United States—Case studies. I. Title. II. Series.

LC4091 .A76 2001
371.826'94—dc21

00-053826

∞™ The paper used in this publication meets the minimum requirements of American National Standard for Information Sciences—Permanence of Paper for Printed Library Materials, ANSI/NISO Z39.48-1992.
Manufactured in the United States of America.

This book is dedicated to the memory of my grandparents,
Fanny and Benjamin Lipschits, who taught me the
power of education against oppression.

Contents

Foreword

The human spirit, if given half a chance, can defy enormous odds. It can overcome hopelessness and conquer abuse if given encouragement and achieve greatness if given opportunity. Society can learn a great deal about the power of the human spirit from Dr. Aronson's deeply moving book, *At-Risk Students Defy the Odds.* She explores the lives of seven individuals who, despite youth marked by poverty, isolation, and adversity, triumphed over cultural, racial, physical, or mental barriers and often within oppressive environments. As she delves into their deeply personal histories, she searches for the secrets of their success and deftly transfers that knowledge to all who have ever questioned the potential of the nation's millions of children labeled "at risk."

Rich in detail, Dr. Aronson takes the reader on these young people's journeys out of fear and desperation to remarkably different lives filled with accomplishments. Each individual points to catalysts that sparked the will to climb out of his or her harsh reality.

I was particularly struck by the story of Ray, a man with mental retardation who never knew his parents and was institutionalized until he became an adult. Dr. Aronson vividly describes his institutional life as that of a "prisoner," subjected to abuse and neglect, and dulled by routine. His involvement in Special Olympics "gave (him) a chance to just be proud . . . and feel good about (himself)," he told Dr. Aronson. "People with disabilities think they are limited," he said. "That's not true. You can do a lot more if you put your heart into it."

From my thirty-three years of work with Special Olympics and the extraordinary youth I have met, I know that Ray is right in his belief in determination. And Dr. Aronson is accurate in her perception that there are actions that we can take, individually or as a society, to reduce the risks of failure. I know that if people are given the chance to develop their potential, they will do so. If they are encouraged, they will push harder to excel. And if they are instilled with love and recognition, people previously condemned by society to isolated, unfulfilled lives can make substantive contributions to humanity. They can become public speakers, program producers, board directors, coaches, and exceptional athletes, as they have through Special Olympics. They can run marathons and bring warring nations together on playing fields of sports, as they have done through Special Olympics. They can become the "social pioneers" whom Dr. Aronson describes in her book as those who journey against all odds . . . to conquer unknown territory." This book and the stories of these men and women are highly recommended reading to all who have given up on our so-called at-risk youth as academic or social failures and to all who care to have a hand in changing their destiny.

—Eunice Kennedy Shriver

Acknowledgments

I wish to thank many people who contributed to this work.

Valerie Sutter and George Thoms first encouraged me to enroll in the doctoral program that, in turn, led me to this book. UVA Curry School of Education faculty Eric Bredo, Jennings Waggoner, Diane Hoffman, Harold Burbach, Mike Caldwell, Bob Covert, and Walt Heinecke considerably diminished my European cynicism, and broke down the stereotypical views I had about the United States, by teaching challenging and thought-provoking courses.

Balvinder Sandhu and his staff provided invaluable assistance when I first started my research.

Anne Knudsen transcribed all the interviews with diligence, intelligence, and professionalism. Patricia George edited the research study that led to this book, and suggested many valuable improvements.

I am greatly indebted to the seven respondents, Vince, Mark, Lori, Lynn, Ray, Renée, and Mary who agreed to relive painful memories and share their past with dignity and insight, in order to give others hope. Without them, this book would not exist.

I am grateful to my husband, John Callaghan, for his unwavering support as I embarked on the study that led to this book. His feedback challenged me, allowed me to sharpen my focus, and led to many engaging discussions. This book exists in great part because of him.

Finally, I wish to thank authors who taught me to always question the status quo, and influenced my way of thinking about education and society, including Jonathan Kozol, Mike Rose, Ray McDermott, Richard Rodriguez, Ted Sizer, Deborah Meier, Victor Frankl, Michael Katz, Stephen Jay Gould, James Anderson, and many others.

Preface

I grew up in the '50s in Algeria, a country where schools educated two kinds of children: those whose parents were European—mostly French—and were destined to become the dominant class; and those whose parents were native Algerians, poor and were destined to become the servant class. Education reflected the social and economic order of a typical colonized country, and this dual system followed its course until circumstances favored a change in the balance of power. Unrest developed and turned into a full-fledged Civil War, which culminated in the independence of Algeria in 1962. The dominant class packed its suitcases and went on to other colonies, or simply back to France, my family and I among them. Although originally from the Netherlands and Belgium, my grandparents and mother had benefited from the colonial system by developing a thriving business of selling trousseau items to the future brides of the dominant class. On the boat that took us away from Algiers, watching our Lady of Africa recede in the background along with my childhood memories, I could not understand what had led us to that moment.

After years of living a privileged life, my family and I arrived in France, where different economic circumstances made the family business obsolete. For the next five years, we barely escaped homelessness. We lived in hotel rooms and ate what we could afford. I was a good student, but poverty dominated my life; I was ashamed of it, and I tried to conceal it from my teachers. In school, I made myself invisible. I had nightmares about books and supplies to buy, teacher–parent conferences, and invitations from friends I couldn't reciprocate. During those years, I began to understand what might have triggered the War of Independence in Algeria.

Later, as a teacher, I witnessed the unspoken dual educational system: education for the privileged and education for the disenfranchised. When I arrived in the United States, I saw a similar pattern and developed an interest in this phenomenon. Who succeeds in school? Why? Who falls through the cracks? What about those children who, somehow, have the ability to cross the glass ceiling of educational achievement? What makes them different? What common explanations are offered for their success?

This book is about those children. It is based on a cross-case analysis of seven successful individuals who grew up in poverty. They represent a diverse array of experiences with respect to historical and geographical contexts, racial and ethnic backgrounds, sex, age, and even academic accomplishments.

Chapter 1 discusses the role of education in a democratic society, and frames the issues of success, failure, and resilience in the larger cultural context of the United States.

Each of the seven respondents has a unique story of resilience that has been life changing for him or her. I am fully aware that their experiences, while individual in nature, also reflect a social and collective experience. In an effort to do justice to both, I decided to tell their stories in the form of semi-structured narratives—something between a report and an analysis. This is what led to chapter 2, in which the narratives are divided into sections that represent salient issues in the respondents' lives.

Chapters 3, 4, and 5 outline the results of a cross-case analysis of the seven individuals' stories of resilience. Chapter 6 offers a number of recommendations based on the lessons learned from the respondents' stories, and looks toward the future.

It is my hope that the stories of these remarkable individuals will inspire many others to overcome the odds against them. I would also like to think that it will inspire educators, policy makers, and all of us to foster resilience among underprivileged children, and close the achievement gap along class and race lines.

• 1 •

Success, Failure, and Educational Resilience in American Schools

> It is not that America is poor. We remain the richest country in the history of the world. We choose, however, to spend our money on our private lives and not on our communities. Those who have some money are given the means to get more of it, and those who don't have an even harder struggle to catch up. The result is the emergence of two Americas, one rich and one poor. The existence of these two Americas defines us, expresses our values, defines our collective character. It is the great American embarrassment.[1]

The reception area of the library in Washington, D.C., has high ceilings and glass walls. Ray's job is to receive books purchased by the library and prepare them for shelving, and the receptionist calls him out of his storage area on the intercom. I look for him among the people who walk by, trying to guess what he might look like. All I know is his voice and the few details that a common acquaintance has shared with me: Ray has conquered tremendous barriers as a child and young adult. Suddenly he is there, an African American man in his early forties, moving casually toward me, a bright smile illuminating his face, his hand out ready to shake mine. We move to a quiet area of the staff lunchroom, where his interview starts. As he reveals his story, his smile stiffens like a mask and the pain of memory emerges from his dark eyes. Ray never knew his parents; his mother gave him up for adoption, and he started his life in a foster home. Shortly afterwards, he was diagnosed with mental retardation and institutionalized until he became an adult. During his childhood, he lived the life of a prisoner. Abuse and neglect were commonplace at the institution, yet, somehow, he managed to survive and turn his life around. Who would have guessed that Ray would eventually conquer the enormous barriers facing him at the beginning of his life? What and who helped him beat the odds against him? Many others in his institution, children like his own sister, did not survive. Why did he? What lessons can we, as individuals, families, communities, and a society, learn from Ray's experience?

I have come to regard people like Ray as social pioneers, because they personify the journey against all odds that men and women undertook to conquer unknown territory. Social pioneers make a symbolic journey from poverty, isolation, and adversity to knowledge, success, and achievement. This book relates the stories of seven individuals who conquered adversity and became successful in their own ways. It is based on a study I conducted from 1998 to the end of 1999. In addition to Ray, six former at-risk students shared their life stories with me in semi-structured interviews.

Vince is an African American man who grew up in a family of sharecroppers in rural Mississippi in the '50s and '60s, at a time when American public life was dominated by racial segregation. As a child, he witnessed the birth of the Civil Rights movement as well as the retaliation against it.

Lori experienced extreme poverty in a white family in rural Georgia at about the same time as Vince. Very early in school, she was diagnosed as legally blind, but her family did not have the resources to help her. Raised in a family where education was not a high priority, she struggled to succeed in school despite her immediate environment.

Renée, a white woman in her thirties, grew up in the Midwest, first in a rural area, then in the ghetto of a big city, and endured years of physical and psychological abuse in the hands of her own mother. She was the epitome of the invisible child.

Lynn is an African American woman in her early twenties who grew up in a subsidized apartment complex with her mother and siblings. Her father was absent and her stepfather was in jail. Her mother-led family, low socioeconomic status, and minority classification made her what is commonly called an at-risk student. In her story, she reveals what barriers she had to overcome and what inner and outer resources assisted her.

Born and raised in Pakistan, Mark arrived in the United States as an eleven-year-old boy and was given to the custody of an uncle. For several years, he lived without his parents or siblings, making on his own the difficult journey to cultural adaptation that many immigrants must undertake when they reach their destination.

Born in Bolivia, Mary, now a young woman in her early twenties, also had to experience the painful linguistic and cultural journey from her homeland to a foreign land, in pursuit of a better life. In addition to financial barriers, Mary also suffered from her father's absence, played a parental role in her family, and developed a consuming desire to adapt to the American culture.

This book describes how Ray, Vince, Lori, Renée, Lynn, Mark, and Mary managed to overcome their oppressive circumstances in many different ways. They all started in poverty, a factor that has been consistently associated with lower achievement in educational research. In addition to poverty, they each had at least one more barrier to overcome, making success in school highly improbable. Vince and Lynn certainly had very different childhoods, yet they perceived their racial identity as a handicap in the eyes of others in mainstream society. Mark and Mary had the added barrier of being immigrants and belonging to a cultural and ethnic minority. Lori had a physical disability, Ray had a mental disability, and Renée was the victim of child abuse.

Notwithstanding their turbulent beginnings, they managed to improve their lives. In view of these barriers, their success stories become highly significant, not only in and of themselves, but for millions of other children currently struggling in American schools. These social pioneers bring a message of "hope and fear," to borrow an expression used by Vince. They bring hope to other children living in dire conditions in inner cities and remote, rural areas, as well as in suburban, public-housing complexes. They also bring fear because success, their stories tell us, requires support systems. As a country, we are currently faced with difficult choices regarding the education of our children, especially our underserved children. We have just entered a new century marked by uncertainties about equity issues in American schools. Let's now turn to those schools and examine the role and power of schooling in our society.

THE GREAT EQUALIZER

Education is often regarded as the most critical institution in our democracy, perhaps because of its transformational power from ignorance to knowledge, from victimization to empowerment, or simply from despair to hope. Education plays a fundamental role in ensuring social mobility. By doing so, it guards and protects the delicate balance between change and status quo necessary to the survival and preservation of a democracy.

Conversely, an educational system that reproduces poverty and wealth across generations creates a two-tiered society, where those in positions of power remain so and those at the bottom of the social scale lose hope of ever changing their lives. Such an educational system threatens the tenets of a democratic society.

Access to public education for all did not occur in America until the twentieth century, and could still be questioned today. A number of educators, historians, social scientists, and researchers have documented that, far from offering equal opportunities to all, schools create more barriers for disadvantaged students by separating them from other students, or by holding lower expectations for them. These discoveries are not new, of course, but they reveal a tension between our professed beliefs and the social reality we allow to exist. For instance, many Americans in 1954 believed that education truly provided equal opportunities for all, until the Supreme Court ruled in the famous case of Brown vs. Board of Education that separate schools for black children were inherently unequal.

Inequalities in American schools did not stop with the 1954 Supreme Court ruling; disparities still persist. In *A Nation Still at Risk,* an education manifesto signed by thirty-seven prominent education reformers in 1998, the authors lament the existence of a "dual school system, separate and unequal, almost half a century after it was declared unconstitutional." They warn the general public that education has become the next civil rights issue: "Too many disadvantaged and minority students are given shoddy imitations of real academic content, today's equivalent of Jim Crow math and back-of-the-bus science." Thus, instead of providing a mechanism to compensate for inequalities among individuals, schools have aggravated them in many instances. The result is a quasi-caste like social system in which the children of advantaged families are given the best opportunities to succeed and the best positions in the social stratum, while the others lag behind, thereby reproducing patterns of social inequality.

As we step into the twenty-first century, the gap between our egalitarian ideals and social reality seems to be widening. On the one hand, schooling is still expected, at least in theory, to be "the great equalizer," a meritocracy by which individuals are sifted and screened for success and failure regardless of race, gender, social class, or minority status. On the other hand, far from jump-starting disadvantaged students, American public schools are losing many of them. Pushed out or ignored by teachers and administrators, these students lose hope, fail, or drop out, and end up in jail or at the lowest paying jobs in the country.

EDUCATIONAL RESILIENCE

In this context of social immobility, disadvantaged students who manage to beat the odds against them have been labeled resilient. Educational resilience has become the object of many studies. Historically speaking, the term resilience first appeared in the first half of the nineteenth century and Webster's dictionary explains it as "the capability of a strained body to recover its size and shape after deformation caused especially by compressive stress."[2] One can surmise from this definition that the word was born in the field of physics. The word was borrowed by the field of developmental psychopathology to refer to individuals who were able to overcome odds against healthy psychological development. In other words, individuals who should have behaved in a pathological way, but did not, were considered resilient. The word then traveled from the field of psychology to the fields of sociology and education. A common definition of resilience is "successful adaptation despite risk and adversity." This definition assumes a universal pattern of human development as the benchmark for "successful adaptation." In other words, I am resilient if I avoid pathological behavior that would have been predicted by a certain set of circumstances (risk and adversity).

Educational resilience has provoked mixed reactions. In moderate circles, it is used as a confirmation that, indeed, everyone in America does have an equal opportunity to education. After all, if some "make it" despite the odds against them, then everybody can, with a little effort. It must mean that our democracy works, and what works should not be changed. The implication of this view is that responsibility for success lies within each individual, regardless of circumstances.

In more conservative circles, the concept of resilience is irrelevant, because of the belief that differences in intelligence—therefore academic success—are genetically determined along race lines. The reasoning goes like this: since success and failure are predetermined, there is no reason to spend any resources on trying to change what is inevitable. At best, resilient individuals represent those few cases at the leading edge of the bell curve, the exceptions that confirm the rule.

In more progressive circles, the predominant response has been to cheer at the emergence of what is seen as a new social tool to equip at-risk students against failure. Thus, even though the responsibility for success ultimately lies with the individual, it is the role of social institutions like school or family to offset the effects of obstacles faced by students, and to make them competitive with their more privileged peers. This approach implies that resilience is something that can be measured, fostered, administered, even inoculated like a vaccine, into at-risk students to ensure their success.

Thus, the questions that have dominated the discourse on resilience have focused around whether resilience is innate or acquired, whether resilience can predict academic success in at-risk students, and whether resilience can be considered a vaccine against failure. If so, what factors can strengthen resilience in individuals or in groups?

The idea of educational resilience became popular in a context of shrinking resources for lower socioeconomic status groups, of an emerging two-tiered society, and a general climate of social and economic laissez-faire. In this climate, where policy makers have been concerned with saving tax dollars by cutting welfare education programs for disadvantaged students, the emergence of educational resilience as a possible predictor of academic success for lower-income students should not be seen as simply fortuitous.

From a philosophical standpoint, the recent interest in educational resilience has a striking parallel to the philosophical debate over intelligence that dominated the field of education and social sciences throughout the twentieth century. In his famous book *The Mismeasure of Man*, Stephen Jay Gould unveils the role of science in the service of dominant philosophical and social policies, and helps us to understand the ideological assumptions behind so-called scientific objectivity. It is not inconceivable that a debate of the same magnitude might take place in the near future over the issue of resilience.

From a philosophical perspective, it would also be interesting to explore resilience with other intersecting concepts. Since there is no resilience without adversity, the word adversity can designate very different situations. It can simply represent necessary milestones in human growth and maturity, or it can designate life-threatening circumstances. Does resilience have the same properties in either case? "Bouncing back" is also somewhat of a fluctuating notion. Does it refer to behaving in a "normal" way, or does it refer to simply surviving trauma, with possible psychological side effects? These questions show the complexity of the concept of resilience and call for correspondingly complex answers.

Other disciplines can shed new lights on the study of resilience. Anthropology of education is interested in the relationship between culture and education and how each influences the other. What role does education play in the dominant culture and how does education change culture? Among working-class achievers, the anthropological perspective seeks to discover what place resilience occupies in the continuum between success and failure and in the dominant culture. Cultural anthropology makes us mindful of what we often take for granted as natural, but is, in fact, a product of our culture. Two social researchers, Strauss and Corbin, warn their colleagues against the insidious effects of cultural assumptions.

> Assumptions that are based on cultural perspectives are especially difficult to recognize because everyone of the same cultural heritage, for the most part, thinks the same way so that no one is likely to question you for making these shared assumptions.[3]

Finally, it is interesting to note that resilience is being closely examined in other modern democracies. In 1999, France held a national conference on resilience, which indicates a similar trend toward explaining and studying the issue. In Asian cultures, especially in Japan and China, resilience is not seen as a tragic necessity, but instead as a positive force to encourage and develop in children at an early age. There is no perceived necessity to protect the individual against adverse conditions. Perhaps resilience of a few individuals amidst at-risk peers does not have the same importance in Asian cultures because individuality may not be as central as it is in Western societies.

The merit of all these perspectives consists in reframing the discussion over educational resilience. That is, in attempting to address these questions, one gains a broader perspective, which can only benefit and inform research. They allow us to unveil unspoken assumptions about resilience.

WHAT OTHERS HAVE SAID ABOUT AT-RISK YOUTH AND RESILIENCE

Many authors have written about resilience, either based on their own research or on their personal experiences. I found the following observations particularly relevant to this work.

In all his books, Jonathan Kozol reminds us that decades after official desegregation of schools, schools in the United States are still fundamentally unequal in their distribution of financial and human resources, and still segregated in their ethnic composition. It is a paradox of mainstream American culture that equality be so much a part of its dream, and so little a part of its social reality. With Kozol, we are reminded that success and failure in American schools are still correlated with social class and race. Therefore, any research on resilience among at-risk youth needs to account for larger contexts. As a society, we need to face our responsibility in offering unequal opportunities to American children. Educational resilience among low-income students would not be such a salient issue if we made different social, cultural, and ideological choices.

In *Ain't No Making It,* Jay MacLeod conducted a field study in a low-income housing development to find out how social inequality is reproduced from one generation to another in America today. Through interviews and observations of two groups of youth at Clarendon Heights (one white and one black), MacLeod unveils how dreams of social mobility are kept at bay for these young people, and how they resist—and at the same time internalize—a system which denies them high aspirations for their lives. Even those few who "make it" to college eventually drop out because they feel culturally alienated from other college students. MacLeod himself reports the difficulty he has in adjusting back and forth from the culture of his university to the culture of Clarendon Heights.

In *Educational Opportunity in an Urban American High School: A Cultural Analysis,* Patrick McQuillan reveals the results of a five-year ethnographic study in an urban school. His study concludes that schools—instead of acting as conduits to social mobility—push away and deny students of urban centers their right to an education. McQuillan blames American culture's preference for individualism, behaviorism, and excessive optimism for not recognizing its systemic shortcomings.

Stephen Jay Gould did not study resilience or at-risk students, but he wrote about a topic that bears on the issue of resilience. *The Mismeasure of Man* is a combined historical study and scientific refutation of biological determinism as it manifested itself in nineteenth- and twentieth-century America. Gould had an advantage over other scientists: in addition to having made a career in science, he became interested in the history of science. This historical perspective gave him the ability to recognize the social contexts in which scientific theories arise, and to unveil the assumptions frequently concealed under pseudo-scientific theories, such as the hereditarian theory of IQ or Polygeny.

Scientists, Gould asserted, can be guilty of three undesirable tendencies: reification (conversion of abstractions into putative real entities), quantification, and ranking. Indeed, these three tendencies have been part of our cultural heritage. Their purpose has often been to justify social inequality among races, social classes, or genders, and to perpetuate social injustice. Gould quoted Charles Darwin in an epigraph to his book: "If the misery of our poor be caused not by the laws of nature, but by our institutions, great is our sin"—showing that science, far from being neutral, has often worked to legitimize inequalities through "the laws of nature."[4]

As we look at what makes a person resilient, we are tempted to consider resilience as a specific feature, either innate or acquired; then, depending on our ideology, we may be tempted to rank at-risk people from most resilient to non-resilient, or we may create a resilience-generating program for at-risk students. In either case, we would commit the same errors scientists made when they attempted to quantify, classify, and reify intelligence. The parallel between resilience and intelligence is indeed striking, and, in that sense, Gould's work is most relevant to this book. We can learn much about the dangers of distortion associated with the desire to rank—ever present in the history of our country. Intelligence, an abstract and complex set of mental manifestations, was (and still is, in some circles) reduced to "a thing in the head" that can be assigned a number for the purpose of justifying social inequalities. The same danger applies to the notion of resilience.

Gould noted that, from a statistical perspective, there is in research a real danger in confusing correlation and causality. Just because two or more measures vary in concert with one another, it does not necessarily follow that one causes the other. Indeed "the vast majority of correlations in our world are, without doubt, noncausal."[5] This provides a word of caution as we study and research resilience in at-risk students. It will be difficult to provide evidence of what causes one person to be more resilient than another. It points to the complexity of the concept and to the difficulty involved in any attempt to measure it.

From Gould, we learn that it is necessary to refer to the social, historical, and cultural context in which a phenomenon takes place. For instance, Gould reconstructs forgotten links, and identifies the consequences of the hereditarian theory of IQ with the rise of Nazism in Europe and immigration legislation in America, and the devastating consequences of this pseudo-scientific theory for the survival of Jews attempting to emigrate from Europe to the U.S., or for the lives of African Americans as they are ranked lowest in the intelligent quotient scale.

STORIES OF ADVERSITY AND RESILIENCE

Victor Frankl provided one of the most striking accounts of resilience. Frankl quoted Nietzche to illustrate his own story: "That, which does not kill me, makes me stronger."[6] Born in Austria, Frankl lost most of his family, including his parents and wife, in the extermination camps during World War II. He survived Auschwitz. In *Man's Search for Meaning,* Frankl gave an account of his daily life and survival along with other prisoners in Nazi concentration camps, and the lessons he learned from it. His tragic experience led him to the creation of logotherapy, a therapy based on understanding the meaning of one's life.

Retrospectively, Frankl analyzed the different stages of human response to the horrors of life in a concentration camp. What happens to men and women who are subjected to the daily horror of being deprived of such necessities as food, warm clothes, shoes, water, hygiene, of a sense of safety about one's life, of dignity, communication with the outside world, or one's family, subjected to beatings and abuse?

Using his own experience as a case study, Frankl defined three stages of mental response to subjugation:

- Shock (an abnormal reaction to an abnormal situation is a normal behavior)
- Relative apathy leading to emotional death (as a protective shell)
- Depersonalization (after liberation), loss of ability to feel pleased, and the need to relearn it

Frankl's book is relevant to resiliency research in several ways. First, it gives us an extreme example of resiliency: whoever survived extermination camps is presumably remarkably resilient. What helped Frankl and others survive gives us an insight into what constitutes existential resiliency (intense spiritual life, the capacity to fantasize a different reality, a profound need to understand the meaning of one's experiences—however grim—for one's life).

Second, few would dispute the assertion that Frankl is one of the most resilient people of the last century. Even though Frankl's core message is not about resilience, his observations have deep significance for anyone engaged in research on this topic, since he himself embodies the concept under study. Finally, having both Jewish and Austrian ancestry, his view on resilience stems from a different cultural context and perspective, enriching it and giving it more depth.

His message about resilience can be summarized as follows: resilience is not about ignoring or avoiding pain at all cost. Understanding the meaning of one's life can offset the effects of adversity and trauma. It is in our consciousness, then, not in engaging in certain behaviors, that we can transcend our hardships.

> To the European, it is a characteristic of the American culture that, again and again, one is commanded and ordered to 'be happy.' But happiness cannot be pursued; it must ensue.[7]

In extreme cases, a good explanation for resilience is pure chance. Frankl never placed himself above others to explain his survival. His own wife died in a concentration camp, as did millions of others just like her who, one day, were sent to the gas chambers for no specific reason. Things determine each other, but "man is ultimately self-determining."[8] With this assertion, Frankl affirms humankind's ability to resist the worst conditions.

In his autobiography, *Hunger of Memory*, Richard Rodriguez offers a different insider's perspective on resilience. Born and raised in a poor immigrant Mexican family, he began his education in the U.S. barely knowing any English. *Hunger of Memory* describes his rewarding yet psychologically painful journey from a modest but warm, loving home to a successful career in academia. In keeping with MacLeod's findings, Rodriguez describes the gap between home life with its intimate atmosphere and a successful academic life, cold and impersonal—two worlds (low-income, working-class home and school) that never meet. Torn between the two, Rodriguez chose school and public life over his private family life. Torn between two cultures, he chose mainstream America over his Mexican roots.

Resilience in his case, while bringing him the academic success to which he was aspiring, also put him in conflict with his own culture and language. Students from lower-income families must, according to Rodriguez, sever their cultural ties with what feels familiar. Resilience, then, comes with an irreparable loss of part of oneself.

Novelist Toni Morrison gives us yet a new dimension of resilience in her novel *Beloved*. Set in rural Ohio a few years after the Civil War and the emancipation of slaves, the story centers around African Americans (Sethe, her daughter Denver, and Paul D.) trying to build a life of freedom after having known slavery all their lives. As in *Man's Search for Meaning*, Morrison's characters somehow have survived the most tragic adverse circumstances one can be subjected to, and now they must start building "normal" lives in a world still hostile to them. The character of Beloved in particular, whether a ghost or the devil itself, symbolizes the losing struggle for normalcy after being forced into abnormal circumstances.

From Morrison, we learn that resilient individuals and groups have a lot of "un-doing" to do, a lot of painful memories to relive and release, before their resilience bears fruit for them. Resilience, then, is not just about bouncing back, but a process that can take many different directions. Sethe, for instance, cuts her own baby's throat and leaves it for dead in order to stop her master from taking them back into slavery. In an extreme case of tragic irony, this infanticide is what it takes for him to stop and for her to escape to freedom and life. Like *Hunger of Memory*, we encounter the theme of sacrifice and loss necessary to gain access to a non-pathological environment. Thus, resilience tells us more about environment and institutions than about individuals.

As their stories will reveal in the next chapters, all seven social pioneers are living examples of educational resilience. Does this mean that they were predisposed by birth to being resilient, or rather that something in their environment helped them to push the barriers? What share of responsibility do others have? Who or what built their capacity for survival and perseverance? The answers to these questions lie in the depths of their life stories.

NOTES

1. Theodore Sizer, *Horace's Hope* (Boston: Houghton Mifflin, 1996), 26–27.
2. Frederick C. Mish, *Merriam–Webster's Collegiate Dictionary, Tenth Edition*, (Springfield, Mass.: Merriam–Webster, Inc., 1997).
3. A. Strauss and J. Corbin, *Basics of Qualitative Research, Grounded Theory: Procedures and Techniques* (Newbury Park, Calif.: Sage, 1990), 1–92.
4. Charles Darwin, *Voyage of the Beagle*, quoted in S. J. Gould, *The Mismeasure of Man* (New York: Norton, 1981).
5. Gould, *Mismeasure of Man*, 272.
6. Victor Frankl, *Man's Search for Meaning* (New York: Simon & Schuster, 1984), 89.
7. Frankl, *Man's Search*, 140.
8. Frankl, *Man's Search*, 133

• 2 •

Seven Stories of Resilience

This chapter gives voice to the seven individuals who agreed to share their life stories with me. The narratives intentionally contain ample citations by the respondents to give the reader insight into the participants' individual stories and viewpoints. All names of people and places are pseudonyms to protect the individuals' privacy.

VINCE

> I've never felt that I was owed anything but a chance.

Family Background

Vince was born in rural Mississippi in 1948, the sixth of seven boys. His parents were sharecroppers, growing predominantly cotton. Vince and his family lived in a farmhouse owned by whites.

> And, in exchange for the use of the land, you shared half of the profits with the owner of the land. So, you literally worked for half of the profits, which you generated. When I was old enough to remember what those profits were, they were roughly $2,000 or so a year. Which means that we lived, a family of seven, well—a family of nine—on anywhere from $2,000 to $2,500 a year, in the '50s and early '60s.

Because the family had such limited resources, food and clothes were sparse. They survived by growing vegetables and raising farm animals. Vince came to understand his parents' struggle to survive at a young age.

> After a certain age, the struggles of what your parents were going through you could just see it.

Work was an important part of Vince's family life, and was divided among the family members. Vince's father worked in the fields, his mother worked in the house and took care of the vegetable garden and farm animals, and the brothers helped with both in addition to schoolwork.

Vince and his brothers were expected to work their fair share around the house and in the fields. As early as age six, Vince started helping around the house.

> And we all had—after a certain age—a farm responsibility, usually between six and seven, you know, depending upon how mature you had grown at that point. And most started, several of us may have started at five or six. But it was mostly six or seven that you're expected to assume some responsibility of the farm. And a lot of it was the harvesting as well as taking care of the plants as they were growing.

Years when the harvest was not good were particularly challenging.

> Those were the real tight years. Those were the years sometime you had to make do with the shoes that you had the previous year. If indeed you had not grown to the point where you simply couldn't wear them. Nothing to wear shoes that were a little bit tight on you. Because you just had to deal with it.

School Experience

Vince's parents went to school through seventh or eighth grade, and could read and write. As the second-to-youngest brother in the family, Vince felt that he had more opportunities for education than his older brothers did.

> We all started school on time with varying degrees of readiness and varying degrees of motivation. Some hated it, you know, others took a liking to it. And, I can't say that there's very much of a difference in terms of the age, but some of us perhaps had more, you know, opportunity for exposure.

All the children were expected to help out during harvesting. At first, schools accommodated that need by holding a summer session that ran from July to mid-August, then closing until November, but in the early '60s this changed and students were required to go to school in September. As a result, most children in rural areas simply missed school for the first three months of the academic year.

> You just had to jump right in there and if you were behind you were behind. And go for it. We did have an opportunity to get the schoolbooks early on, to the extent that we could. We could do reading at night by ourselves, but you know, you lost a lot.

The school Vince attended had eighth-grade graduation, since many students did not go beyond that.

> My eighth-grade class was between 95 and 100 people. My graduating senior class was 43, a 50 percent drop-out rate.

Vince remembers his first-grade teacher.

> She's still alive today. Her name was Ethel Simpson. One of the most even-tempered, easygoing, caring, lovable person I've ever met. You also knew to draw the line. Because she could also discipline you but didn't have to. Because of the way she carried herself, the way she'd handle you, very few people would get out of line. She made the classroom so interesting to you. Even the layout at that time was really child-friendly. How she presented herself as a teacher, and storyteller, and all those kinds of things, was absolutely wonderful every time. And, I think that that was a motivating feature for us all.

One of the most powerful role models in Vince's life was his third brother who went on to college, graduated, and came back to teach in Vince's school.

> The fact that he was in college. The fact that he graduated. The fact that he came back. And the fact that he was respected in the community was something to really look up to.

Vince was an intelligent and capable student but unmotivated until he reached tenth grade. His teacher, sensing the potential in him, started provoking him by drawing comparisons between him and his fifth brother, a very capable student. It worked. Vince applied himself more to his schoolwork and improved his grades. "You get hooked to it." From there, thanks to a scholarship, he went on to college to study political science and economics, then on to graduate school at the University of Illinois.

In graduate school, Vince started feeling the effects of what he had missed during elementary school.

> I suffered from that in graduate school and have limitations, you know, even today. I had to study five times more than the folks that were around me. They just sort of got it. And I had to work at it. When I produced a research paper, I had to spend a heck of a lot more time at it to get it near the quality of the other people that were around me. That was more pronounced at the University of Illinois than at Tulane because all were basically African American counterparts to myself around the nation. So, the real exposure to competition was really at the University of Illinois, and it took me a while to start getting it.

Racial Segregation

Vince grew up at a time when all public institutions were racially segregated.

> There were black schools and white schools. And the access to the basic school materials and equipment and educational as well as athletic programming were limited in the African American schools—pretty limited. No football. They had basketball. No baseball. No softball. So basically the only sport was basketball. You could not sit at a lunch counter. You could not go into a drug store and buy a cone of ice cream and sit at the counter and eat the ice cream. You could buy the ice cream but you had to take it outside.

Asked how he felt growing up with unequal access to almost all services in the community, Vince answered:

> Very, very bitter. And you felt very threatened, you felt bitter about it. And I have to say, you also felt inferior. . . . There is, I don't care how much you fight it . . . an inferiority complex that develops around it. And it's very difficult to fight it off. And subconsciously it's going to be there.

For African Americans, social life was reduced to:

> Three things basically: there was a basketball game at the school; it was meeting downtown on Saturdays; and there was church, you know, on Sundays. And, that was basically it, in terms of your social experiences. They were routine, social experiences in the little town.

For Vince, poverty and racial segregation were tightly connected.

> I mean the segregation and what had happened historically, you know, caused—in a large part—poverty. And I don't think there can be any doubt in anybody's mind. That's what it was.

Civil Rights Movement

By the time Vince was in high school, the Civil Rights movement was underway. Vince has vivid memories of that period of time, and credits the Kennedy administration and the leadership of Civil Rights movement for ending legal racial segregation.

> The speech that John Kennedy made about the admission of James Meredith to the University [of Mississippi]—where he talked about the disparity between blacks and whites—and that there was no reason for that to continue to happen, was quite encouraging. I think that's probably one of the defining moments in my life in terms of what I wanted to do.
>
> The success of things like the march on Washington in 1964 . . . those things were uplifting and they were motivating. You didn't gain a lot immediately economically, but the real benefit was hope, you know. That was a motivating force.

But he also recognizes that the law changed faster than the mores, especially in the South. As a result, with hope came fear.

> Don't ever forget the fear, like when you have something like the death of Chaney and Goodman in Philadelphia, Mississippi—and that's not very far away from where you live—if you have those kinds of things happen and you read about the lynching and you also know that there are a lot of them that took place that you don't read about—because it doesn't make the paper—that's, that was very frightening. And that raised a tremendous amount of anxiety. I mean, crops were burning and those kinds of things were very, very common. And, there was nothing to when you went to your church on Sunday morning and there was a cross that had been burned on the church lawn.

Poverty

Both poverty and racial segregation resulted in limited access to things that the rest of society had access to. But for Vince, poverty was stronger in limiting access to material commodities. For instance, his family did not acquire electric appliances until the late '50s.

Yet Vince said he never was aware of being poor.

> Yes, we were limited in terms of our physical resources, you know, physical ownership of things—clothing and whatever—yes, we were limited. But I don't ever remember going outside of the house when I wasn't clean. And although we had limited dollars, I don't ever remember going hungry. I'm sure I didn't get what I wanted to eat all the time, but I don't remember going hungry, you know. Sure we were limited in terms of educational opportunities, but we did get into school every year and were supported very strongly by our parents in that.

Despite their poverty, Vince's parents managed to give him a strong sense of security. His father was a church leader. He credits his mother with creating an additional source of income by selling eggs and milk products from the farm and growing products so the family would not have to buy them.

> Those helped with the income situation—filled some holes there with the income situation. She was very judicious about that. And I saw that quietly in what my parents represented. My parents were not vocal people, but they had a lot of quiet strengths and determination that things could be better for us.

Achieving Despite the Odds

In Vince's opinion, resilience results from the combination of natural abilities and exposure to new opportunities. He therefore supports social programs that improve the environment in which children live.

> I think it's a combination. I really, really do. You are, in my opinion, as a result of being given physical health as well as no latent mental defects, have some natural abilities. . . .
>
> All of us have seen people with a lot of natural tendencies, natural abilities, that don't excel at all. . . . That's why I think that certain types of investments with families and individuals are so important . . . . I mean things now like Head Start. So, just some basic exposure to things, you know, offers people hope. And that's why, you know, you can talk about low-income barriers and, for instance, some of the technological barriers that exist now, it's why it's so important to do. Because access to information and the quality of that information does allow some people to catch on.

What Vince lacked in basic content knowledge he more than compensated for in social sensitivity.

> I think I am probably more knowledgeable about interpersonal relationships than most people around me are. I think I'm probably more knowledgeable about being sensitive toward the issues that others face than perhaps people that are around me.

Looking Toward the Future of Children Living in Poverty

Vince is both hopeful and cautious about the future of children living in poverty.

> Hopeful in that the opportunities are greater, with the exception of certain isolated areas around the country. There is more of a safety net there. And the quality of a public-supported education system in most areas is better now. Although you hear all kinds of negatives, they are better than when I grew up. That doesn't mean that they are anywhere near where they should be, because they're not.
>
> On the other hand, the number of kids that are in poverty now that are growing up without intact families is absolutely frightening. See I had—and most people around me had—not only intact families, but also extended families.

Families, according to Vince, were a large part of the support system that helped him and others achieve despite the odds, and to simply "keep them out of trouble." This support system is no longer available to most children growing up in poverty.

> And it's not there anymore. And that is why I think we have the rate of crime that exists in a lot of our inner cities and our communities around the country that are actually wiping out a substantial portion of the future, in low-income communities. Not only black communities, although the black community is impacted by it more significantly. So, although the quality of things has improved, the exposure to information has improved, the ability to get a better education is there, some of the social and family issues are the major concern now. And, you know, and that's what leads me to say that there has got to be massive investments in support of families around this nation.

Community support systems have become essential in order to improve the lives of children living in poverty. Rural poverty will be more difficult to address than urban poverty.

> Even poor urban areas tend to have more resources. State governments are more supported and advanced in investment in education in urban areas than in rural areas. The educational leadership and political leadership are far more informed and aggressive in that respect. There is more parental knowledge. There are significant issues of parental participation in urban areas across the country. But, generally, the parental participation is of a higher quality in knowledge.

Because the ability of local governments to supplement what the state governments contribute varies tremendously,

> A lot of localities can't do very much to supplement the basic and that substantially lowers the quality. I mean, you want to talk about the technological barriers, that's where it's going to be more pronounced in 2000 and beyond, because we are nowhere near technologically literate in those small towns as kids are now when they are in fourth, fifth, and sixth grade. It just doesn't exist. And you talk about computers in homes, you know, I heard on TV that maybe 30 percent of American people have computers in their home. I would bet you in my hometown it's less than 5 percent.

Despite these blatant inequities, Vince is convinced that capitalism is the best system in the world. He feels optimistic about the future.

> My hope lies in the newer corporate leadership, which will be prepared to make some investment that improves social imbalances. Because I think that they're thinking more and more about the work force of the future. And there may be some opportunities to bridge some of the inequities in the educational system. At least I hope so.

Vince praises President Clinton's strategy to combat poverty and inequalities.

> I think his strategy is right to engage corporate people that really have the ability to have something happen. Make something happen both at the government level and in their communities because they have a tremendous amount of wealth. You know, Microsoft, one-half of a trillion-dollar company.

Opportunities

The time has come to stop placing blame, Vince suggests.

> I've never felt that I was owed anything but a chance. You know, really. And I still feel that way. You know, I'm acutely aware of the impact of

> discrimination, the impact of prejudice, and what that does to you. My chance is my opportunities. I'm extremely aware of it. And I think an awful lot of people need to be more aware of those. But it's not good enough to sit around and say, "You owe me." That's not the solution. The solution is to try and move through and work around those prejudices and those constraints.

He issues an appeal to the African American community and its leadership.

> But I just want to emphasize again, things like drugs and the breakdown of the family, and the rate of incarceration of my people . . . it's frightening. It is absolutely frightening. That to me is what our leadership has got to focus on. The leadership of traditional community and civil rights organizations has got to focus on this issue a lot more than they have in the past. Otherwise, the American Dream is going to get further and further and further away. So the dream can be realized, but you got to work like hell at it.

LORI

> I love to serve the people everybody has given up on.

Family Background

Lori was born in 1949 and grew up in the mountains of north Georgia, an area she compares to West Virginia in its poverty, except that most people in Georgia were farmers rather than coal miners. Lori's family did not own land, and Lori and her cousin were the first in her family to graduate from high school. Lori's parents were married when they were fifteen and sixteen. Four years later they had their first child; Lori, the second child, was born when her mother was twenty-one. A third child was born three years later. Then, when Lori was five years old, her parents divorced.

Within a year or two, Lori's mother remarried and one child was born from this marriage. Lori's step-dad, who went to school through first grade and a few days in second grade, was a lumberjack and earned $2,000 a year. After a year or so, he took a job as a school bus driver, and then stopped working altogether.

With no education beyond a couple of weeks in seventh grade, Lori's mother had no job and stayed home until a dress factory opened its doors in town and she got her first job.

> It was a dress factory or sewing factory. She worked there for a couple of years, then a shoe factory came to town and they gave her more regular hours and so she changed to the shoe factory and she worked there actually gluing insoles in shoes for twenty-seven years. She developed a degenerative neck disease because of sitting on a stool and she had constant bronchitis because of the fumes from the glue and it was not an air-conditioned or air-filtered room.

The family survived by growing vegetables on a piece of land that Lori's uncle owned, and with help from her mother's relatives. During those years, Lori lost contact with her father.

Under pressure from her relatives, Lori's mother remarried for material stability, although her new husband, instead of providing sorely needed income, proved to be an additional burden to the family.

> I think when we were really young, it was probably okay. By the time we were middle grade, it wasn't okay, and he and my older brother fought a lot. I don't think I resented my stepfather, truthfully, until I got old enough to realize that he was sitting there and my mother was killing herself.

When Lori entered first grade, the school discovered that she was essentially legally blind, a condition that no one in her immediate surrounding had noticed about her.

> I was always straining and going to sleep after about an hour at school so they took me in for an eye exam and the health department bought me glasses. I had a patch on my eye and they did all kinds of strange things, but I was lucky that I didn't have to have surgery because it had gone on so long.

The environment in which Lori was raised was devoid of intellectual stimulation.

> I grew up in a home with no books; well, we actually had a Bible and a hymnal, and then in high school a World Book Encyclopedia guy came through the mountains and sold every poor soul a set of World Book Encyclopedias which I don't think we ever really used. And those were our books. We never owned a children's book. First book I ever owned of my very own was when I went to college and I bought textbooks and books to read.

When her mother started working at the factory, Lori took on many parental responsibilities.

> From the time I was eleven, I was cooking the dinners at night and doing the laundry, carrying the water for the washing machine for a family of six, and of course, my brother helped, but men's jobs were defined very differently than women's jobs.

The family seemed fairly close except for:

> Some real animosity with my stepfather, particularly as we got older, because our mother had to work so hard and, you know, he wasn't. So, some real anger and animosity there.

Homelessness

After her parents separated and before Lori's mother remarried, she remembers a period of vagrancy, during which her mother and the three children would stay with relatives for a while, then move on to others.

> They were all poor. So having a family of four come in to live with them when my mother was producing no income was really an additional burden.

During that time, the family was staying with Lori's uncle when, one day during church, some neighbors announced that the house was on fire.

> And we actually went and stood there and watched the house burn and fall to the ground. There was no fire department in the county, nothing. So we watched what few little tiny possessions we had totally burn up. So both families were now homeless and we went to live with relatives.

Caring Adults

While life at home was austere and grim, a few people in her life helped her. Her grandfather, for one, truly cared for her. Lori's mother used to say, "He thinks the sun rises and sets on you."

Lori's grandfather did not encourage her to pursue an education or to do anything special. He just doted on her, and loved her no matter what and "that really began to validate me."

A few teachers emerged as caring adults in Lori's account. Her fifth-grade teacher

> was funny and she was a mom who was just real laid back and who talked about her family lovingly and you could see her laughing in the halls with the teachers and I was thinking, you know there's a different life out there. Because, I mean, I have a family for whom survival is a big issue. And here are people who literally come to work and relax and enjoy it. So that was a big thing. And, I don't remember a lot about sixth grade except that I remember she was real touchy, she would put her arms around kids and if they were sad she would talk to them, not feel sorry for them but just bring a smile to their face.

One of her teachers, Miss Darla, was Lori's honor society advisor and taught her Latin, algebra, geometry, and trigonometry. Miss Darla became Lori's mentor in school. When Lori was invited to join the honor society, she could not afford the $4 fee.

> I didn't have the money so she said, "Well, I will help you. I will lend you $4, but you have to work it out. Bring whatever you're going to bring for lunch; you can't eat in the cafeteria." I couldn't afford to eat in the cafeteria anyway, and she knew that. "Come to my room and you'll clean my classroom because the janitor doesn't do a good job. For six weeks you have to do this for the $4." Well, I thought it was a great bargain! Four dollars was like a million to me. So, every day I'd go to clean. I'd be cleaning her chalkboards and doing dusting and stuff, and she'd come in and say, "Okay, come on, you have to at least have your biscuit and whatever you brought from home." So, I'd sit down and eat and she talked to me about life, and that God had given me this gift of, you know, brains, that I should use them.

Later, Miss Darla encouraged Lori to apply for college,

> I didn't even know what college was when I was in the tenth grade. She said, "Why didn't you raise your hand that you're going to go to college?" They gave everybody the PSAT because I guess we fell into some category where they could do it for free. "You did real well on the PSAT, why aren't you going to go to college?" And I said, "Because I don't know what college is."

School Experience

Lori's first-grade year was traumatic. She entered first grade (there was no kindergarten or preschool) totally unprepared.

[I] went to school, did not know how to tie my shoes, did not know what my birth date was, did not know my address, a lot of things that kids know at three and four in this area, and certainly when they go to preschool. Didn't know how to tell time or anything. I was furious. I came home from school the first day absolutely livid, crying and crying and yelling at my mother, I can remember it as if it was yesterday. Saying to her, "How could you send me to school without my knowing these things?"

Following her diagnosis, her "good" eye was patched to force her to use the other eye. She often felt "in the dark," yet, her first-grade teacher was very nurturing and caring.

I was just being overly exhausted because it was so much strain in terms of learning to use an eye that you've never used. And then learning to use glasses and kind of coping with the world in a different way.

From second to fifth grades, she never spent the entire year in one school.

There was a lot of anxiety, tremendous anxiety I would say, around moving and adjusting to new schools and feeling different. Second grade, I remember that was probably one of the poorest years of my life in terms of just not knowing if we were going to have enough food and all those issues. And, I think I had four different teachers in the second grade . . . because of moving.

Lori has no recollection of third grade. "I don't know who my teacher was, and I'm not sure where I was." By fourth grade, things started getting a little more stable because they stopped moving.

I had a wonderful fourth-grade teacher. . . . I came to the fourth grade with essentially no self-esteem. I remember doing geography and it was so traumatic. She gave us a map of the United States that was blank and we had to fill in with all of the states and places. Well, it meant nothing to me. The United States meant nothing to me, you know. I mean, there was nothing outside of this little mountain county. And so I just remember becoming frozen and then hysterically crying. So she sent me to the bathroom, told me to wash my face, get myself together, that she would help me to do it.

And, she finally took me outside and said, "You can do this. You are very smart. Everybody who's had you in their classes for three years before this say how smart you are. And you are going to do this and I am going to help you. But you're going to do it." I remember that being a big part of my fourth grade. And it was a change in terms of how I started looking at things.

By the end of the seventh grade, Lori felt very comfortable. Her teacher was the principal of the school, and often put Lori in charge of the class when he had to tend to administrative tasks.

Of course, I didn't need more responsibility; I had tons at home. But being validated outside the home was different.

In contrast, the first two years of high school (eighth and ninth) were a nightmare.

It was really very, very painful. I was probably, if not the smallest, close to the smallest, person in school; I hadn't gone through puberty; I didn't go through puberty until I was probably at the end of the ninth grade. I was really very tiny and was kind of underdeveloped, so that didn't help with the self-esteem, and the thick glasses. I was socially inept at fitting into that kind of environment with that many grades at once and wandering in the halls, I was terrified. You know, changing classes and going to lockers and all that kind of stuff. So, it's a blurred nightmare with real insecurities and all the kind of things associated with that.

Academically, she feels that her high school prepared her well in math and English, even though it did not offer much in terms of electives. However, when she entered college, she felt behind in many areas, due to previous lack of exposure.

I couldn't have gone to Duke University. I think that the cultural shock would have been too great.

Her mentor, Miss Darla, helped Lori apply for school and a scholarship, and soon Lori was accepted in a junior college. There was a lot of resistance against college in Lori's family. Her mother did not want her to leave, and never acknowledged her daughter's academic achievement.

She certainly didn't give me any present. I don't think she ever even mentioned the fact that I graduated. I think probably on the one hand she was proud of me that I was smart and I went to school, but didn't understand why I felt I needed to go to school.

Lori's father, however, reacted differently.

> I guess to go back to high school graduation, my real father came to my graduation and bought me a set of luggage. All during college I wrote to him. And so we developed a communication, and I didn't trust him because my mother didn't trust him. But I got to know him. He died in 1992 of a brain tumor, and I spent a lot of time those last months taking care of him. And, it was interesting, he knew far more about me than my mother did and I lived with my mother. Because he valued every piece of morsel that he picked up.

After her undergraduate degree, Lori went on to Duke University and earned her M.A.T in mathematics.

Lori's co-curricular activities in high school were virtually nonexistent, because of limited resources and her parents' perception that such activities were frivolous. Fortunately, she had a friend whose parents would pick Lori up to attend a game from time to time.

The Community

Lori's experience of high school is not disconnected from home. She did not feel part of two different worlds, because there was virtually no income or social class gap in her community. Everybody was poor or low-income working class with the exception of teachers and attorneys. No one was extremely wealthy.

> This was not so much "the haves" and "the have-nots." Everybody was poor, pretty much. The farmers were struggling because they had to take their products across the mountain and they had to get products from across the mountain. I don't remember growing up, for example, with fresh fruits and produce in the market, in the little tiny grocery stores, just because it'd be rotten by the time it got there practically.

Until Lori's mother got her job at the factory, the family had no health coverage.

> When I was really small and I was very sick a lot, my mom actually had to take me to the next county to the hospital. I mean, we had no health insurance, so she certainly wasn't going to take me to the doctor if she didn't need to. If I got really, really sick and she couldn't get the fever down, then I would go to this Dr. Ed, who would give me a shot of

> penicillin. . . . Then, once my mom started to work, she had health insurance for us, after sixth grade, I guess.

Distancing Herself from Her Family

Because the county where she lived was so remote and mountainous, there was no diversity of population. Therefore, Lori grew up totally unaware of the system of racial segregation that existed at the time ('50s and '60s).

> When I went to honor society, Miss Darla took me to Atlanta. It was my first exposure, first time I'd ever been around a black person at all, and I was so naive. We went in to get a soda from a soda fountain—which I'd never done before either—so we went in, there was a whole gang of us, and I plopped down on this stool by this black girl and I started talking to her and she was so rude to me. So rude to me, and I was just was taken aback. And I thought, "Oh, well, this is different."

Back home, she discussed the incident and discovered her family's racial prejudice.

> I think a great chasm between me and my family happened at that point because my mother said something to me about blacks, and I said, "Well, you're going to be really shocked when you get to heaven when we're all there together." And she said, "Oh no, God's smarter than that. He'll make a black heaven and a white heaven." And I thought, "Oh, my God."
>
> So, at that point, I knew that there was this chasm which I would never cross again; we were intellectually and values-wise so far removed.

Building Her Own Family

Lori met her husband in undergraduate school. They were married days after graduation, and moved to North Carolina. She studied for her master's degree while teaching. In 1974, after her husband got his Ph.D. and his first job, she followed him to California. After their first child was born, she continued to teach part-time and wrote a teacher's manual for metric math. The couple moved back east, and Lori soon was pregnant with twins.

> And so I stayed home and did volunteer work. A lot of volunteer work. And took foster kids into my home.

Organizing Her Own Ministry

Asked how she became executive director of Community Service, she explains:

> Well, I actually started Community Service in 1988. I guess because I had stayed home and had done a lot of volunteer work and helped start a Mission Church and took foster kids into my home, I was very much aware of the needs in the community. And I was serving on a nonprofit board that was working with street people and was asked to talk about what the needs were in the county and the problems and what should be done about them. I only came to the meeting to answer questions, but here I am. I started brainstorming and thinking out loud about what the issues were and what the gaps in services were and decided to do something about that. I really didn't intend to start Community Service as an organization but it really was my ministry on the streets. And, it soon outgrew me, so I needed an organization to help support the work, you know, to do more of the work.

The organization is now in its eleventh year. Community Service seeks to build strong families and safe communities by improving the quality of life of impoverished men, women, and children. It does this by offering programs that respond to their individual physical, spiritual, and emotional needs. Community Service offers services that address short-term as well as long-term needs (food, housing, health care, transportation, education, etc.). A few years back, Lori received an award for her work at Community Service. A video was made, and when she went to visit Georgia, her niece asked her to bring the video, so that the family could see it. Her mother did not seem to be interested. She found an excuse for not watching it.

> It's four o'clock in the afternoon, right, and my mom said, "No, I need to stay around here and fix Will (that's my step-dad) a little supper because if he doesn't eat right at five o'clock he gets sick." Well, I don't know if my step-dad said something to her, or she thought better of it, or somebody else said something after I left, but she walked in. She came to the door, she and my step-dad, and they stood in the doorway, but without coming inside the door. The video played for five minutes, it was playing when she got there so it was less than five minutes, and my niece was asking me questions, "Why was this done?" and all this kind of stuff. But, my mom didn't even stay to listen to these questions. As soon as it was over, she said, "I guess I'll walk back to the house" and she turned around and walked away.

Lori thinks her mother doesn't show interest for what she does because she is intimidated by what she doesn't know. Lori's family has rarely visited them in thirty years, and when they do, it's for less than a day.

Going Back

Lori sometimes goes back to Georgia.

> For a lot of years when I'd go back, I'd be really depressed when I'd come back because it was so depressing to see how poor and uneducated they are and that they haven't done anything about getting out of that situation. But, once I started accepting it, it's still hard; I mean, I work with people who are low income and homeless, and my mother qualifies for USDA surplus food. You know, she doesn't know I know she's getting it, but I can recognize it when I open the refrigerator. There's butter that's USDA, you know what I'm saying? I'd never say anything to her about it. It's kind of like going into a time warp.

Role Models

Still, Lori credits her mother for being a role model in her life.

> My step-dad certainly didn't model anything that was much of any value, but my mother was a very strong woman. Obviously, she had her own issues, but she was loving and nurturing in many ways. She didn't know about building self-esteem and those kinds of things, but she certainly set forth a model of hard work and has always modeled that for us in terms of getting out and really busting yourself to do whatever you need to do.

What Helped Lori Succeed

Lori feels that a combination of factors helped her succeed, despite the odds against her: first, role models, and then, caring adults. She credits her grandfather who always loved her, not for her success in school, but for who she was as a person.

> And I think that's probably one of the most beneficial things that can happen to people in their lives is to have somebody who thinks you're absolutely terrific.

Lori also cites her faith.

> My faith has always been a very strong part of my life when I felt like everything else failed. It was a very substantial source of strength to me. And I think—this is a really strange kind of thing to say—but I really think from the time I was very small that I felt there was some kind of mark or touch on my life that meant I had to do something responsible. And, I don't think I could have articulated that particularly until I was older, but I knew I was different. There was sense of understanding that I was different, and I don't mean that to say, "Oh look at me, I was great," and it wasn't that at all. It was just feeling like I was different, and I don't know how to say it except that. From the time I was really young, I mean, I would say two or three years of age, there was a real kind of inquisitiveness and questioning of what's going on in the world, and what's beyond this little town, and are people all the same, and things like that. And I remember driving my mother nuts because I'd ask questions all the time. She says out of four children, I was the most difficult to raise, and yet I was not a person that ever needed a curfew or had gotten in trouble. And so I think that there was obviously a work for me to do and for whatever reason there was a call in my life, I guess, I don't know. It's kind of a strange kind of thing to say, but that was something that was different from the beginning. But I've always kind of felt like that; never knew quite what it was.

Making Sense of the Past

When looking back at her past, Lori feels like her whole life was a preparation for what she's doing now.

> The years I was home with my children I knew that I did not want to go back to the classroom and teach and, not that I wasn't a good teacher and didn't love it, but I just knew that wasn't what I was supposed to do the rest of my life. But, I didn't know what it was. So I went to a local college and there was like a six-week class that graduate students offered on, I call it, "Finding out What You Want to Be When You Grow Up." It was a battery of tests so they evaluate them. It was interesting because everything I had in common was I had most in common with a priest, the president of a company, a counselor, a social worker, and a teacher. And those are the five areas that I need at Community Service.

Poverty, explains Lori, left her with whole pieces of her education missing.

> I feel like there's a whole piece of my education, even now, that's missing, because I wasn't exposed to a lot of stuff. And I'll never catch up. I feel like there's always a deficit in some of those areas. The poverty and the lack of education in our family were certainly a thing. I know that by the time my kids were in third or fourth grade I think they were probably as sophisticated in terms of worldly things as I was by the time I got through college. I mean, it just took so long, I've played catch-up my whole life. So, I think that's a real negative.

However poverty also made her a survivor.

> So I think it's positive in that sense that I know that I'm not going to get anywhere or do anything without having to work. And I think one thing that became very obvious to me in high school was that if I feel different and I am different in terms of my thinking, and I'm going to chart another course for myself, it will never be easy.

Education gave her a greater advantage over some of her siblings. Also, moving out of the area helped Lori in a very significant way.

> I think the other thing that's helped me to be really successful is moving out of the area, away from the family, because it's so easy to just go there and have no motivation and have, you know, the same kind of sheltered life. My siblings did not move away. My sister, recently, but not before.

Asked what it takes for children living in disadvantaged settings to succeed, Lori answers that besides food and shelter, a minimum sense of security, and motivation, creating some sort of relationship is essential.

> And I think there probably has to be some external resources brought to bear on the situation. There's some advocacy and some push from the outside, because it's not going to come from the inside.

Hope for Everyone

Lori's difficult childhood made it possible for her to understand and form relationships with those people who are outcast and destitute. There is hope for everyone, she affirms, even those "everyone has given up on." In that sense, her past has significantly influenced her present life.

Lori defines the American Dream as becoming the best person one can be, but not necessarily as defined by society's standards.

> I don't believe we should try to make everybody middle-class Americans. So that, our homeless people, we don't try to make them people who are going to work at IBM. We have them understand that they don't have to do what I'm doing. One of my clients said to me the other night—came up to me and gave me a big hug and I said, "Are you still working at K-Mart?" And she said, "Yes! I love it! This is my fifth year!" . . . And her oldest kid is going to college this year. She's just so proud and, you know, she's done that. I really believe that everybody can have a dream, and I don't think we should set a standard for everybody.

RAY

> Coming up a big hill.

Early Childhood

Ray was born in 1958 in Washington, D.C., and was placed in a foster home shortly after birth. Ray has very few memories of his early childhood.

> I remember very little. I remember just always crying a lot because I always felt something was wrong and I didn't know what was going to happen. I always felt that.

Concerned with Ray's behavior, his foster family took him to be tested at an institution for children with developmental disabilities.

> There were some things that they noticed that I wasn't doing, I wasn't on level with. And I had a very hyperactive problem where I couldn't sit still.

Diagnosed as mentally retarded, he remained in that institution and was subsequently transferred to City Home, an institution for people with disabilities run by the city's government, which became known for its history of abuse and negligence.

> And I stayed until I just got older, older, older, and when I wanted to get out they'd let me know that I wasn't coming out until I learned something from that institution. I lived with about 300-something people in one cottage and all of us had mental retardation, various types of disabilities, so we all were set in that one little site until they found out other programs.

Ray spent his entire adolescence at City Home until it closed its doors in 1978. He then joined a group home under the administration of the city's human services.

Ray doesn't know his father. If he were to meet him now, he says he wouldn't be able to accept him.

> I have an aunt that tells me about my father and how great he is and, still to this day, I wouldn't be able to accept him. My mother, you know, I know she's passed on but I don't think I would be able to accept her either.

Life at City Home

When he arrived at City Home, Ray discovered that his older sister and brother had been residents there for years, and they all met for the first time. Shortly after his transfer to City Home, the three siblings were informed that their mother had passed away.

> It was kind of sad to go to her funeral and you've never seen her in your life.

When asked what he had to say about City Home, Ray answered:

> It was an institution that had a lot of, I guess you could say, it had a lot of goals. But a lot of the goals they had we weren't very happy with. We were treated more like we were prisoners, like we had committed a crime. And what I found out through all that was that they just didn't know how to really work with us, because of our disability.

Despite the abuse and negligence, Ray says he became used to this type of life. He recalls an instance when some relatives offered to take the three children (Ray and his siblings) home for Christmas week. He looked forward to spending the holidays in a real home, yet was totally unable to handle the change.

> I cried the first day I got there. I cried so loud, so bad, that Friday I was back in the institution. I was more frightened not knowing really what was going on here. I'd been in two institutions and I still didn't know what was going on. And someone, one of my family members—my grandmother—said to everybody, "Send him back. If he wants to go back, take him." So, they took me back and I felt sad going back because they were really trying to show me some love and I didn't have it.

Ray talks about the staff's common lack of knowledge with regard to mental disability. Some children had severe disabilities, and when they'd get upset, they would start crying and screaming. The staff controlled them through heavy medication, just as they did with Ray's sister, who died under strange circumstances.

> She had a disability and when she got upset, the only way they could control her was to give her heavy doses of drugs . . . and when you'd see her she was just a zombie until that stuff wore off. And one day they told me she had passed.

Asked what he thinks happened, Ray answers:

> I don't know. I do know that she had a blue spot in her hand. That if you would see it, you could tell that something was wrong with that hand. But they didn't take the time to even touch it. They waited about two or three weeks and then started reacting. Where the hand was getting bluer and bluer and bluer, it was broken. They put a cast on it. More medication. It was more than she could handle. But for me, I wasn't supposed to know all that. I was just supposed to know that she died from a heart attack.

Abuse was routine at City Home. The abuse was perpetrated by staff and by residents.

> Some other client may have a grudge against someone, something silly. . . . It could be a small thing. That's why we did have to fight. I had to defend myself because one time I had the whole cottage upset at me. And they grabbed me and said, "Well, we gonna take care of you. We know what to do with you." They put me in this closet. They locked the door. They left me in there from 7:00 until 11:00.

Residents were grouped by race and by degree of severity of disorder in different cottages. Most slept in dormitories; a few "old timers" had private rooms. After many years, Ray became "captain" of his dormitory, a function used to fill the gap left by a shortage of staff.

> With me being captain means that I'm responsible for making sure that everybody cleans the dormitory—really the staff is supposed to do that.

Friends and Enemies

At City Home, Ray had a few friends with whom he is still in contact, and he married a former resident of City Home. Ray also had enemies—people who just didn't like him. As an example, he cited a newly arrived resident.

> Like the guy that loved to set fires. He'd call the fire engines and watch them come by to put out the fire. That turned him on. And we'd welcome him to the cottage, you know, but he would have a grudge against everybody in the cottage because he couldn't get to start that fire that he wanted to start or he couldn't get his way with it. And, there'd be times when I may be in his way and he'd just say some words that would provoke me to go beat him up. I was wild then. "What did you say?" But, I didn't touch him because I knew he had some serious problems.

Fights among residents were frequent at City Home. Ray admits he fought frequently, even though fights were usually followed by punishment, and even if the staff was involved with or provoked the fights.

> Well, there were times when I would joke with them and they were not in a joking mood. And then they would chase me down and if they could catch me, they probably would beat me.

When residents misbehaved they were sent to "Hemlock."

> Hemlock is like jail. It means that if you get to the point where you get out of line and out of control where you break windows, and your behavior becomes very, very bad, they have to put you away. Now it's called a detention center, but then it was called Hemlock. You broke a window or you got caught doing something that you weren't supposed to, they'd lock you up in Hemlock. Basically, Hemlock is a place where it's just like jail. It's a real jail.

Fights and punishments, as well as uncertainty and a sense of insecurity, contributed to fear and a sense of looming danger.

> Sometimes I felt afraid because I didn't know what was going to happen. And you really don't know what's going to happen day to day.

A Typical Day at City Home

> [We'd] get up at 5:30 in the morning, staff walking in and yelling, "Get out of bed! Get up!" Like we were almost soldiers. So, we had to get up, wash

> up, clean up, dress up, line up to get ready for medication, those who were getting medication. Those that weren't getting medication, we'd line up again, straight line—sometimes by two, sometimes by one—and we'd head off to the cafeteria for breakfast. Right after breakfast, we'd come back to the cottage, and for those who were going to school, they were sent off to school. We walked out as a group to school. And for those who had appointments, they'd go to their appointments. Then we'd have lunch, go back, and finish up the day. And then we'd come back to the cottage. Sometime we had to clean up and get ready for dinner. So we'd go back down and get our dinner. And then after that we had a time where we could go back out and play basketball, sport time. And then after sport time, shower. We had to take a shower; something was wrong with the pipes. If it was just cold water, you'd take a shower with cold water. That's it. If you had warm water, you were lucky, but everyone had to be showered and then after shower we had to go to bed. That was a day at City Home.

Ray found solace in the thought that despite the negligence and abuse, others at City Home were worse off. Other children, those with severe disabilities, were never allowed outside the institution, whereas residents at his cottage could sometimes go out.

School Experience

Currently, at age forty-one, Ray reads at the fourth-grade level, having improved by one grade level since the last time he was tested. He says he would like to be at the twelfth-grade level. He presently attends evening classes at the Kennedy Institute.

> I'm trying to get back a little bit of . . . a lot of the education I lost when I was there.

Needless to say, school was a difficult place for him. Classroom situations were particularly stressful because he felt behind in most academic areas, such as reading and mathematics. Ray's favorite subjects in school were nonacademic: sports and music. "Everybody loved Physical Ed. . . . You'd get out of class." In sports, he enjoyed the sense of competition, which would force him to focus his attention. Music gave him a setting to express himself, as Ray loves singing and acting. In fact, during our interviews, Ray often enjoyed portraying different people as they talked to him, producing a certain comic relief to an otherwise very sad story.

A few fond memories of teachers (mostly those who were kind to students) soften the harsh memories of school in general.

> We had a very good music teacher, and she was a little different than a lot of these other teachers. She had children with disability; she made us feel good about ourselves and music. We enjoyed performing. We had two guys who were blind playing banjo. She was just an amazing person. I was able to get in there, I tried to sing a little bit and I was a little too loud, she told me to bring it down a little bit. But she was exciting, you know, and you didn't get to see that. And many people wanted to stay and hang out with her.

At the age of sixteen, Ray and a few others were given the opportunity to attend special education classes outside City Home, something he considered a breakthrough.

> When [City Home] was able to work with the city, they were able to take some of us that were in institutions out of institutions to mainstream them into regular schools in the city so we could get used to jobs, learn how to get a job, what it takes to get a job, stuff like that.

For the first time, Ray said he felt "normal" in a school setting.

> I was happy to get to see new people. I didn't have to do the same old dull thing, you know. Just the same thing, over, and over, and over.

Through the special education program, Ray was introduced to a volunteer job at a municipal library, where he was later offered a full-time paid job, and which he still holds to this day.

Feeling normal felt good for Ray, but for some of his peers, it created a sense of shame. Boarding the bus that would take them back to City Home after school, some would hide at the back of the bus

> because they didn't want other people that were in the school to know that they had a disability.

Ray never felt that way and would question his friends, "What are you doing that for?"

Getting out of City Home

When he was fourteen or fifteen, Ray got his first summer job.

> I got a chance to work in a store and I didn't know how to cook or anything, but I ran orders and stuff and someone showed me how to cook short orders.

In that job, he was given more responsibilities than he had ever carried at City Home and his self-esteem started improving.

Finally, under a federal court order, City Home (and many similar institutions) was forced to close its doors in 1978. Ray and his fellow residents were getting out. "It was a good year," he says.

> I could maybe get out to see what the community had, and I know the community would be glad to see me get out and just be me.

Ray joined a group home through the city human services office. Life in a group home was not what he had expected; supervision was even tighter than at the institution. At that time, he was already working at the municipal library. He described how embarrassed he was when, one day coming back from work, he found himself unable to explain to a cab driver where he lived relative to his workplace. He ended up calling his counselor who came to pick him up.

Ray and his friends from City Home discovered that citizens were not excited to see the institution close its doors.

> When we got out of the institution, we were excited. But the problem was the city wasn't excited. What are they going to do with all those people? You know, and the police department, no one really wanted to see that happen.

Ray then realized that citizens also needed to be educated about people with disabilities.

> And, what I thought after seeing that was, well, what I see is that the city needs to be educated about looking at us as individuals.

Special Olympics

One of the most significant events in Ray's life at City Home was his involvement in the Special Olympics.

> Just going out, competing, and just giving it all you have. And getting a gold medal. That's what I liked about Special Olympics. They gave me a chance to just be proud.

Ray and other Special Olympics athletes enjoyed competing and meeting new people. The organization gave him what he needed most at the time—self-esteem and a sense of achievement.

> People awarding you, hugging you, congratulating you . . . making you feel good about yourself.

City Home had a basketball team that won the championship in 1972. This athletic victory provided the team a chance to go to the International Games. Ray was a track and field runner at that time, and got a chance to go along.

The sense of competition was strong in Ray and he had to learn the fundamentals of winning and losing.

> It wasn't easy for me, because a loss is a loss, no matter how you patch it up: "I lost!" And they'd be like, "Ray, you didn't lose, you . . . come here."

The confluence of Ray's life with the Special Olympics had a major significance for him. The Special Olympics gave him an opportunity to shine that he hadn't had before. Being encouraged, winning and losing, traveling outside the narrow sphere of interaction of City Home, and the interest Mrs. Shriver and her team showed in Ray gave him the confidence he needed to go on with his life.

Ray became a spokesperson for the Special Olympics. He gives regular speeches to different groups, traveled to South Africa as an ambassador to the Special Olympics to encourage the establishment of a Special Olympics group there, and has reached a leadership position within the organization.

> I wanted to stay with Special Olympics because that's what elevated me throughout my life. So, I joined the "SO Fit" team, which is a special fitness team, and I do a little bit of encouraging other athletes. I go out and I do public speaking to the community to tell them about children with disabilities.

The Special Olympics also expanded Ray's horizons and knowledge base in ways that the schools he attended could not do for him. "I'd never, never been to South Africa . . . never really heard of it." Ray is now a recognized leader in Special Olympics, has a steady job that he likes, has been married for fifteen years, and has a son. Asked what helped him reach this unforeseen life, Ray evokes his spiritual side:

> Each time I pray, I know something good is going to happen. And, like my wife, one of her things was her favorite swing—she had a swing at City Home that she called her favorite. She'd go down there, it was on

the ball field and she'd swing and she'd talk to her God about whatever it is she wanted, and everything she asked for, she got. She wanted a husband; she got a husband. She wanted a child; she got a child. Now she wants a house and I said, I don't know if we are ready for a house yet.

Often, he says, people with disabilities think they are limited.

That's not true. You can do a lot more, if you put your heart to it. What I want to do when I leave Special Olympics, I told them, what I want to do is, I want to be able to go back and to work with some of the little children to give them some encouragement. So when they get older they will feel good about themselves. And we hear more and more success stories.

Awards and Recognition

Ray tells of his brief encounter with public officials:

You know what's interesting? I got an award from Marion Barry. We had this big luncheon and they gave me this award and he said, "This award is presented to Ray and his wife for overcoming obstacles in their lives. And they are a model to the nation." And I thought that was really, really nice. A citizen they said, a model for the nation, which is good. I felt good about that. But I was telling my wife, and I was saying, "If we are a model, that means the mayor can give us anything we want." Donna was like, "Nah, he didn't mean it like that. That's a politician speaking."

Revisiting City Home

When asked what the most difficult part of his past was, Ray answered, "not being given the chance to really get a good education." City Home authorities denied Ray the opportunity to be educated because of his hyperactive behavior. "I needed to be supervised." Ray denies having had a serious behavior problem.

I think it was just more of a young kid, hyperactive—very hyperactive—and they didn't know how to control . . . work with that. That's what I think it was.

When he looks back at all his years at City Home, he remembers the school and wishes he had been given a better chance to learn in school. He also remembers the people who didn't come out of City Home (his sister and some of his friends), and feels the responsibility of educating citizens about people with disabilities.

Poverty

Ray's entire life experience unfolded in the context of poverty. Had he not been poor, he would not have ended up at City Home, yet Ray did not experience poverty as an obstacle. He currently lives in a small, subsidized apartment with his family, and is grateful for the assistance he receives from the government.

Understandably, Ray is much more aware of his disability as the major obstacle in his life. He is acutely aware of the disadvantage a person with disability has, but not of the disadvantage a person experiences living in poverty.

RENÉE

> I had decided that I wasn't getting married and wasn't having kids. None of that. I was afraid that I wouldn't be able to deal with it. But, then, what I've told myself now is, I do have the resources that I need. I have an education.

Family Background

Born in the 1960s, Renée lived with her family in a midwestern rural area, and then later in the low-income area of a city after her parents divorced. Renée's parents only dated for three months before they married; her father was nineteen and her mother was seventeen. One year later, Renée was born.

> She (mother) was an abused child herself so she didn't know how to care for me or take care of me. And she basically got married to leave an abusive situation.

Shortly after Renée's birth, her father was sent out of town and the physical abuse began.

> She was alone with me in the country—in the middle of nowhere—with no support system; not quite knowing how to take care of her baby.

> My dad told me that a lot of times he'd come home and I would be in dirty diapers and crying, or have bruises and marks on me, and he wouldn't know. He'd ask her where they came from and there'd always be an excuse.

Renée's first brother was born one-and-a-half years later, her second brother two years after that. One day, Renée's mother woke up her three children.

> It seemed really late to me but it was probably ten o'clock—my mother had me and my brothers get into a car of someone we knew. She took us to a shopping mall and we had to walk through the mall and we got out on the other end and we got into another car and left. And I was confused—what are we doing and where are we going? She wouldn't tell me anything.
>
> And we got to this place, this house, and I asked where we were and she said she didn't know. And I was always very curious . . . wanting to know why all the time, but never really got any answers. I remember just staring out of the window thinking, "Where am I?" You know, just so confused. And then I saw a school bus go by that said Pennsylvania something or other. I realized we were in Pennsylvania. So I went and I told my mother, "We're in Pennsylvania." She didn't want to talk to me; she was talking with some ladies. I was listening in and she told these ladies that my dad was abusing us. And I was just like, "What? That's not true! Why is she lying to these people? She's the one who hits us." I was just really confused.

As it turned out, mother and children returned home after about twenty days, and Renée's dad eventually left the home.

> My mother was not only abusive to me and my brothers, but also to my dad. She used to hit my dad and my dad would never lay a hand on her. He's a very mild-mannered man. He left the house.

Renée remembers the exact day when the divorce was finalized. Her mother received custody of the children and a monetary settlement, and they had to vacate the house, which her dad had built. Before they left, her mother asked the children to vandalize the house.

Perhaps because her father worked three jobs, Renée did not feel poor when her parents were still together.

> He was a farmer, and he worked part-time as a mailman, and he also worked full-time at a machine maintenance shop.

But after they separated, she became intensely aware of their poverty.

> We moved to the inner city, into a low-income housing project. And that's when it first hit me that we didn't have money. We moved into a neighborhood that was predominantly black and we were the only little white kids there. We were scrawny little kids with no clothes, you know, no decent clothes and kids really picked on us a lot and so we pretty much lived in fear the whole time we were there.
>
> When we'd go to the bus stop, kids would beat us up, pull our hair, and just be mean. We were just scared little kids and we didn't know how to defend ourselves. If we would have tried to ever defend ourselves with our mother, you know . . . so, we never were the kind to fight back. At least not then.

Her mother's behavior was unpredictable and irrational. Anything could trigger the beatings: a glance, a gesture, a word, or nothing at all. There was no discussion possible.

> When I was ten, I remember that my mother would go through extremes. One day she would be like a princess—treat us like she was our fairy godmother and just be totally wonderful. And then the next day, she'd be like the wicked witch of the west. So we never knew what to expect when we came home. So we could come home and she could be happy as a lark, "Oh let's go do this!" Or we'd come home and she'd be in a rage saying, "You guys are all getting beaten for whatever." It'd be like, "What do you mean?" You know, and she would just go crazy.

The abuse went on with the added stress of no longer having their father to protect them. Renée and her brothers were repeatedly insulted, slapped, beaten with a belt or other objects, or kicked out of the house. Her mother seemed to suffer from a severe psychological disorder, perpetuating a vicious cycle of violence that had started generations before her. Renée recalls the worst episode of abuse she suffered.

> I remember one time I was about fourteen years old. I was home with the flu for a couple of days, just very sick. But while I was home, she had me cleaning house and babysitting and doing whatever else she wanted me to do for the neighbors. We were not allowed to take a shower without permission. We were not allowed to eat without permission. . . . Everything had to have permission.
>
> So, I had worked all day long doing dishes, laundry, cleaning, cooking, and finally it was about nine o'clock and I said, "Can I go wash my hair?" And she said, "No, go to bed." And I said, "But I have to wash my

hair out." We weren't allowed to bathe in the morning, it had to be at night. I said, "I have to wash my hair. If I don't wash my hair the kids are really going to pick on me tomorrow at school." She said, "No, you are not washing your hair." And I said, "Please." And I probably begged her like four or five times, "PLEASE" . . . begging, just begging.

And, I got on her nerves, I'm sure. She said, "No, you get to bed now." And I said, "Please, you don't understand." I knew kids were going to be unmerciful with me. But she said, "All right, you're going to get it now." She ran up the stairs after me.

She got the belt out and said, "Bend over." I said, "No, I don't need to be beaten for this. This is wrong. No, no, you don't understand! I just want to wash my hair." But she went crazy and I wasn't going to bend over for it, I just kept saying, "No, you don't understand." And she just started swinging that belt at me every which way. I mean, head to toe, just whacking me. She usually doubled it, and I think she started out doubled, but then she just started swinging it, going crazy with it. And then she said, "I'm really going to teach you now."

And then she turned it around and held it by the other end from the belt buckle and then she started swinging that at me. She hit me in the head about five times or so and I was just hurting from head to toe, everywhere. I was just in so much pain.

She said, "You get in bed and I don't want to hear another word out of you." And I got in bed. And I was trying so hard not to cry because when she tells you you're not allowed to cry, you better not cry or you're going to get some more. But then, if you don't cry when she spanks you, she's going to spank you until you cry. I tried that one time—tried not to cry. And she kept beating me until I did cry.

So, I got in my bed and I pulled my covers up and I was just shaking. I couldn't stop shaking because I just hurt everywhere and my head was throbbing. I tried so hard not to cry—I held my breath so I wouldn't cry because I knew she was really, really mad. But, I couldn't. . . . Every time you breathe you whimper . . . and she kept yelling, "I said shut-up." I thought "Oh no, I'm really going to get it." I tried holding my breath.

She started screaming, "You're going to get it now." She came running up the stairs and I thought, "Oh no, she's going to kill me." And then, she came over to the bed and then she went back—I remember, very clearly—she goes back and flips the little light switch on the wall, "You're really going to get it now."

She came over and got ready to start beating me on top of my covers, "Oh no, we're going to do this right." She yanked my covers off the bed. She grabbed my arm and she yanked me out of bed. Then she let out a blood-curdling scream. I wondered what's wrong. I looked back and my pillow was saturated in blood because my head was bleeding.

For fifteen years, Renée endured the abuse, somewhat helped by her brothers' presence. Periodically, social services would visit their home.

> We had social workers out at our house all the time because of child abuse and asking us questions, but they were stupid. My brothers and I would sit in a row—the three of us on the couch—my mother would be standing there . . . and the social worker would ask us questions. We would sit there and lie through our teeth. We were scared to death of her. We knew if we'd tell anybody anything, she would really give it to us.

Renée's mother remarried. Her new husband was a very strange character who lived on welfare, liked to steal from cemeteries, and would send the children to sell products door-to-door.

> He would make us go door-to-door selling whatever he created. He would crochet things and he'd make afghans and little toilet paper dolls and weird things. So my brothers and I—ten, eight, and six—would go door-to-door selling things to people.

He never beat Renée or her brothers, but was violent to their mother. His sexual orientation was not clearly defined and he had gay orgies in the house. The marriage only lasted about a year.

Strangely enough, even though she was only ten or eleven at the time, Renée's mother would talk to her as if to a friend.

> I was like her confidante on one level. And then . . . the other level, yes, so I did have a little bit of leverage sometimes. Since she came to me with all her problems as a little girl, I had some leverage with her. But not a whole lot, you know.

Every other weekend, Renée and her brothers visited their father, who had also remarried and lived about forty-five minutes away. Each time, he would ask her to come and live with him, but the fear of retaliation was greater than the desire to leave her mother.

> And every time we went to see him, he'd ask me—up until I was about twelve—to come and live with him. And I would never answer him . . . because it was just too confusing. You're not sure how to get out of this situation . . . without getting yourself killed. . . . And so you just never did anything about it.

One day, when Renée was fifteen, her mother overheard the children complain about their life with her. She called them in, and asked them one by one, which of their parents they wanted to live with. Out of fear and confusion, her brothers answered "you." But when Renée's turn came, she couldn't bring herself to say what was expected.

> I thought, "I can't lie anymore. I can't take this. I can't stay here." But then I thought, "I can't tell her the truth either, what am I going to do?" I stood there for what seemed like an eternity and she got so mad, because I didn't say a word, I just stood there. She said "Fine, you're out of here! You are out of my family; you're out of my life. I'm calling your father tomorrow while you're at school and you're out of here tomorrow."

The next day, an anxious but hopeful Renée went to school for what she thought would be the last time, said goodbye to her few friends and went back home, expecting to be picked up by her father.

> When I got home I was so happy. I thought, "Yes, I'm leaving." At home, my mother was just sitting there acting normal and I said, "Did you call?" "Call who?" I was devastated. I thought, "Oh my goodness, I can't believe this. Oh my goodness! I cannot believe this." I went from up here to, you know, way down. I was just like, "Oh no." I was just so crushed.

A New Life

The next day, Renée did not go to school. Instead, her mother asked her to watch her friend's three children while her mother and her friends went out. Renée turned on the television.

> The *700 Club* was on and I was watching it and I actually remember the episode, it was something about people who were gay. The man said, "If you're gay, if you're struggling with these issues, call this number." "Well, I don't have those problems, but I do have problems." So I called the number and I talked to one of the counselors on the phone. . . . I said, "But I don't know if my dad wants me anymore, because he hasn't asked me to come live with him for three years. So maybe he doesn't even want me, because he has a new family now."

The counselor took her call and advised her to call her father and ask for help. Before her mother and her friends left, Renée spoke with one of them.

> "Lisa, why don't you tell my mother that as punishment, she needs to send me to go live with my dad . . . and then maybe she'll do it." Oh no, Lisa couldn't use the little conniving way I planned, she told my mother, "Renée doesn't want to live with you anymore, she wants to live with her dad." So my mother came in yelling and screaming—in a major rage, and she started calling me swear words and yelling at me, just saying, "You are just out of my life, I don't ever want to see you again. Goodbye, good riddance . . . you just go live with your dad. I don't ever want to see you." And I was sort of relieved when she said that and then she left. I asked if I could call my dad. . . . I called him collect. I called my dad and I was crying and crying and crying, and my dad started crying. And he said, "I'll be right there, I'm going to be right there to get you!" So, I hung up the phone with my dad and he was there in forty-five minutes.

After a few days in her new school, she was called into the principal's office and her heart sank when she saw her mother sitting there, claiming that Renée had actually run away from home. She was told to leave the school with her mother and not come back. Her mother threatened to take her to juvenile detention.

They stopped at the county sheriff's office, on their way to her father's home, to be accompanied by a police officer. After an hour-long discussion, the officer authorized Renée to stay at her father's until her mother placed a warrant against her. Her mother had to leave without Renée. Renée's father sent her to his dad's until the situation was cleared up. After a few days, her dad obtained temporary custody of Renée, and she was able to go back to school.

> I had to go to court and testify against my mother and tell what had gone on. She sat there and I testified in front of her and in front of her friends and people she brought there. They just looked at me like, "How can you do this to your mother, you evil child?" So none of them really knew but the one lady, Lisa, she knew what my mother was like and she was there the day my mother beat me next to death. And she lied. She got up on the stand and lied and said that it didn't happen . . . my mother spanked me because I was being disobedient. And I thought, "Honey, you don't know what spanking is."

After that, Renée was able to live with her father until she went on to college.

School Experience

In this context of gratuitous and unpredictable violence, one can easily imagine that, for Renée, school was more like an impressionistic painting, a ghostly presence than a strong, supportive environment.

> Fourth grade was a hard year because that was the year that my parents separated and my mother, brothers, and I stayed at a shelter and we were gone for almost a month—probably about twenty days.

Like many other children growing up in abusive homes, Renée knew how to make herself inconspicuous so as not to attract potentially negative attention. As a result, she appeared to her teachers to be invisible, and not deserving of their attention.

> I was a little child, a scrawny little kid. As a child, I was just a kid that other kids made fun of, just because I was little and extremely shy. I wouldn't exert myself in any way. So I would always just keep to myself and not talk to anyone.

Most teachers ignored Renée or wrote her off. A few teachers sent her to the school nurse who would ask Renée if she was being abused.

In constant fear of her mother's retaliation, "I lied through my teeth," Renée explains.

Another source of embarrassment was getting free lunch at school.

> We hardly ever had food in the house. We did get free lunch at school, which helped. It was very embarrassing to get free lunch, because the other kids knew that it was free lunch because you have to give your free ticket and they would just make fun of you for it.

Her mother did not allow Renée to do homework at home.

> She didn't let us do homework, because, she said, "School work should be done at school, not at home."

So she had to sneak in homework, as she explained, with the threat of being beaten if caught. More often, she was too afraid to do it.

> So, I would do my homework in the hallway before class, because the bus would get us there about ten to fifteen minutes early.

As long as she was in elementary and middle school, she was able to maintain decent grades, but when she reached high school, the long-term effect of her mother's absurd dictate and the whole context of Renée's life caught up with her academically, and her grades plummeted to Cs, Ds, and even one F.

> Up to tenth grade, I'd been taking general course classes, nothing challenging at all, because when I was in junior high, everybody knew I was a kid from the projects; nobody encouraged me to do anything, to take any classes that were preparatory for college. In junior high, there were college prep classes you could take. And no one told me to take them, and I didn't take them. If no one encourages you, you don't think of doing that.

When she finally left the abusive situation, her grades started improving.

> I was confused as to what future meant for me at that point, because I didn't know what to do and I never, I never dreamed that I would ever go to college. . . . It never crossed my mind! Someone came to the school from a vocational center when I was in tenth grade, and talked about the vocational school. And I thought, "Yeah, that's interesting. Maybe I could be a nurse," because we talked about the diversified health occupations program. "Well, you know, that might be possible! Maybe I could do that." So, I applied and they accepted me to the program. I said, "Okay, that's what I'll do." So I went to the vocational school for eleventh grade. I got straight As in everything I took and I was just like, "Wow, I am not all stupid" and I was so excited.

The summer before, Renée had undergone back surgery and wore a back brace for half the school year. When the brace came off, her muscles were atrophied and she was unable to do heavy lifting, which meant she wouldn't be able to continue her training. Her counselor suggested college.

> I said, "Go to college? What do you mean?" She said, "Go to college!" And I thought, "No, I can't go to college. How could I go to college?"

With her father's support, Renée eventually accepted the idea of going to college. She went back to her high school to take advanced classes that she hadn't taken before, graduated from high school, and was admitted to a Christian college.

> My first semester was an eye-opener because I still hadn't developed great study habits, because when you haven't done it before you don't know what you're supposed to do and you sort of like not having to study.
>
> So, I thought I could do that in college too. . . . It didn't work very well. I still did okay though. I think I got like a 3.2 my first semester. I took a class called "Music in the Western World" and I did not want to read the text. I got a D in the class and I was devastated. I went to the professor and said, "I'm two points from a C in your class. Can I do some extra credit or something so that I can get a C?" He said, "Renée, you are in college. There is no extra credit. Welcome to the real world." I needed that.

Renée graduated with a bachelor's degree in psychology, and then earned her master's degree in counseling.

As she looks back on her own experience in the school system, Renée offers the following analysis of the effect of school on low-income students:

> I think that teachers need to not look at you as a poor kid, but as a child who has potential. They looked at me as a poor kid. They never encouraged me to do anything. And I think if kids have encouragement or someone to work with them, then they can make it. I think that's a big thing, just having someone believe in them.

Forgiveness

Long after Renée was out of danger, she carried within her feelings of hatred and low self-esteem. She was living a new life with her feelings buried deep down in self-protection. Above all, she could not bring herself to forgive her mother, and it was only through the experience of her religious faith that she was able to do so. In a letter that was published in a Christian publication for teenagers, she described her feelings:

> I didn't want to forgive my mother, since she had hurt me so much, and I claimed to be a Christian and I thought I was. If we don't obey Jesus, we are sinning when God's word says to forgive your brother. I wanted to hold a grudge against her for the rest of my life. But then I decided if Jesus can forgive me for hating her, then I could forgive her for how she treated me.
>
> I put my burden on the altar that morning and I was forgiven. If you hold anything against anyone, forgive him so that your Father in Heaven may forgive you your sins. (Mark 11:25).

It took several years and a number of significant religious experiences for Renée to find the strength to forgive her mother. Today, she no longer feels any animosity toward her.

> I don't think she's a bad person. I just think that she did not know how to cope with the stresses in her life—living in the projects, living in a place where people were violent. There was a lot of criminal activity going on, drugs, alcohol. We lived in a duplex and there was a prostitute in the one connected to us. Just lots of bad stuff. I mean, people stabbing each other, and lots of bad things going on. And we never had enough money. I just don't think she knew how to cope with the situation she was in. And so, when it got really bad, she would go crazy.

Starting Her Own Family

Having seen her mother beat a baby in her care when it cried or could not pronounce a word, Renée vowed that she would never attempt to have a family. Aware of the cycle of abuse running through the family, she simply decided to stop it. Then, she realized that the education she had received in psychology and counseling would be a tremendous asset that no one else in her family had. She married two years ago, and is currently pregnant with her first child.

> One of my concerns was, how am I going to deal with a baby, myself. Am I going to end up just like my mother? But I told myself, "No, you're not!"

Although she admits she would never leave the baby alone with her mother, she has not severed the tie with her, and was actually expecting her mother's visit at the time of the interview, the first overnight visit in fifteen years.

MARK

> As you come from different nations, every country has good and bad things. Adopt the good things; let go of bad things. And teach the good things that you have from your country.

When we started the interview process, Mark was twenty years old. The first interview took place in the fall of 1998 and due to Mark's schedule, continued in an electronic form (e-mail). Mark is now twenty-one and majoring in managing information systems.

Family Background

Mark is the eldest of three (a brother and a sister, both in high school), and lives with his family in a subsidized apartment complex in northern Virginia. Mark and his family are first-generation immigrants from Pakistan. Mark and his father came to the United States when he was in sixth grade. Shortly after they arrived, his father went back to Pakistan and left Mark in the care of an uncle.

> We both came here because my uncle was here. And we came here, and he was thinking of winding down whatever his business was back home and come here and do that here. But, unfortunately, he didn't really like it. My mom and my sister and brother, they were back home too, and so finally then I just stayed here with my uncle and he left.

For two years, Mark did not see his immediate relatives. They finally arrived when Mark was beginning high school. His mother does not work and his father works as a dispatcher at a local airport.

Mark feels very lucky to have the family he does. His parents have always valued education and have always encouraged him to focus on his studies, especially his mother.

> Education is like a very important thing in my family. So, they have really pushed me.

Unlike many, Mark was not encouraged to have a job while in high school.

> And I know people—Pakistani, Indian, American, a lot of people who—students, new students—were working full-time in high school because their parents had bought a house and they all needed to help, and they were to keep on going like that. My parents, they never wanted me to do that. They never wanted me to work full-time. Actually, I never worked when I was in high school.

Adjusting to the United States

When asked why Mark's father decided to immigrate to the U.S., Mark responded:

> Probably for, I would say, better life, more security, and better education for his children.

The greatest challenge for Mark, when he first arrived, was the absence of his family.

> My parents were not here. . . . But I was lucky enough to have my uncle. We really got along, still today. So, we were like friends even when we were all in Pakistan. So even though I kind of missed my family, and my father is his brother, real brother, so that's how he's my uncle. And he also missed the whole family back home, so we were both in the same kind of, in the same boat. He went and told me, "We both miss our family," then because I was here it was a little better for him and because he was here, I didn't really feel like to an extent, where I would say, "Oh, I'm lonely." I had my parents, even though I didn't have them here. And I was, I guess I was lucky enough to have him.

In Pakistan, many speak English, so Mark was at least familiar with the language. In fact, he says he actually understood pretty much what people were saying to him, he just did not speak it. "We studied it over there but we never really spoke it there."

Even though Mark has adjusted very well to the U.S., he still calls Pakistan home. Asked whether his siblings were born in Pakistan, he answered: "Back home, right, in Pakistan."

School Experience

Mark enrolled in seventh grade in a junior high school and was placed in an English as a Second Language class. He describes his first impressions.

> It was really different because the background that I come from or I would say, most other people, well, a lot of people who are from Pakistan or from Asia, we are brought up a little differently than it is over here. So, when I went to the class the first time and I saw, people—a variety of people, they were all from different nations and different countries—and they were not really giving the teacher the respect that I think was important. They were not really listening to the teacher, or they were just into their own stuff. So when I got there and I, first I was surprised why it was happening and then, you know, after two to three days I kind of learned that that's how it was. But it didn't mean that I had to do the same thing. And that, to the teacher, it was different. And, I was recognized for that. And, so that's how it was.

Mark says it was hard for him in the beginning. In an attempt to adjust to this new culture, he tried to be like others.

> It took a little time for me to learn that. But, then I found out that the teachers, they were paying more attention to me, not them. And, as well as I was gaining the love from my teachers, I was gaining the respect, which I thought was the most beautiful thing.

Mark enjoyed the personal attention that teachers seemed to give him. This, he said, only happened in small classes.

> My music classes and mathematics, and even U.S. history . . . that was a good class, I liked all these lectures. And the small classes where I was, the teacher, where I was able to talk to teachers, express myself, it was good. Those were the teachers who were really helping me.

Mark eventually adjusted to his new surroundings and started making some friends, all from Pakistan. Asked how he explains that students in high school tend to stay within their own ethnic/cultural group, Mark answers:

> Let's just say that, we didn't really talk to many other people, we were getting along with everyone fine . . . Americans, white Americans, black Americans, Asian Americans, and Hispanics, you know, Spanish Americans. All of us, we were just fine. It's just that when it came to, well, sitting on our lunch table, we would kind of do, and they would do the same. And that was in high school, but in middle school–junior high we were like all together.

He stayed two years in that school, and then transferred to a local high school for two years. Then his parents and siblings arrived from Pakistan and they all moved to another community.

Caring Adults

Mark's uncle stands out as the most important adult in Mark's early life in the United States. He seems to have taken the role of Mark's father or big brother, which created a bond between the two. Mark speaks very highly of him.

> My uncle, whenever he would go to school and he would really feel proud, that made me happy and to keep on doing how I was, especially with teachers and my studies. So, whenever he went to my school, no

matter if it was the middle school or the high school, he was always happy. And I was happy that he was happy.

Success and Failure in American Schools

Comparing schools in Pakistan to schools in the United States, Mark gives higher marks to the former in terms of education attainment level, but he feels that the American school system is actually better.

> I would say that the level of Asian schools or the level of Asian education is higher than here in the USA, but the system here in the USA is better than the Asian system. First of all, over here we have, the good thing about the United States is that we do have opportunities and a person who wants to study can. It may be a little hard for one if the person is supporting himself or herself—if they don't have like a family who can take care of the rent or groceries or what have you. Then, it's a little harder because the person then has to work full-time and study as well. But, those who have families here who can support them, I don't think there is any problem for them.

Mark explained that, in his opinion, success and failure depend in great part on individual willpower, given that the education system gives you the opportunity.

> [People who fail in American schools fail] . . . because they want to fail. Let's put it that way. Because everyone in school is given an equal opportunity to study and to do well. And, most of us, we don't really have to work full-time when we are in high school. Keeping that in mind, if a person is not going to study, it's because they don't want to study. Maybe because of their friends. Maybe because of peer pressure. Or maybe because they don't find that interesting at that point. And I'm sure that most of us who have the opportunity but do not avail it, realize it after long time, but at that time we can't really do anything.

Another positive feature of the American education system is that it offers many opportunities for continuing education.

> Another good thing about the United States is that whoever wants to study at whatever age, they can do it, which is good. Back home, if a person is older than forty-five years old and wants to go to school, people would be like, "Oh, he's going to go to school now." So that's one good

> thing. But, as you get older, you get more responsibilities and life gets hard as well, so then it gets harder that way.

However, Mark thinks that high expectations are a better feature of Asian education systems.

> The way we are taught in Pakistan or Japan or Korea or what have you, any country in Asia, I would say, most of them teach you in a way that you learn it, forcing you to do your homework, punishing you if you don't do it, which I don't think is right. And the way their exams are structured, the teachers back home they expect you to know stuff. They expect you to put input into whatever they are teaching. And we don't really have multiple-choice exams there a lot. We have to like write essays and memorize and all that kind of stuff. But a person who wants to study, no matter where they are—in the USA, Spain, Puerto Rico, Korea, Pakistan, India, wherever—a person who wants to study will study, no matter where or no matter how.

His favorite subjects in middle and high schools were math, algebra, geometry, and history "because teachers were very nice."

However, when he moved to his second high school, Mark discovered a different culture among teachers there.

> Even though it is the same county, at Fellowship High School teachers among themselves talked with each other about students, how they were doing. Let's say if you are an English teacher and the other teacher is a U.S. history teacher, you would know what I did in U.S. history, so you knew how to handle me. Or you know what my capabilities are. So that, as a group, teachers can teach me better, or they can correct me or my behavior. I really like that. In Community High School, however, teachers were not really communicating with each other for students, and the counselors, they were okay. I had a good counselor because I was being nice to the counselor. It was my way of dealing with people, so I didn't really have problems. But I saw people who were not really getting along. And, overall, the teachers again, well, one of my geometry II, algebra II teacher in Community High School, I didn't really learn much. I still got a B though, but I didn't see that it did any good to me. And the teacher was a very nice person. Some people love stuff but they can teach it. Other people, they know it, but they cannot teach it. I think that was one of the problems, which screwed me for my basic math as well. So, anyway, I graduated from Community High School in eleventh, I didn't go in twelfth. I just did it a year early.

What motivated Mark to graduate in eleventh grade was not only the less motivating culture of Community High School, but also seeing a friend graduate that same year.

> Well, she is doing it. And then I asked my other friend, and all of them they were like "Well, if she's doing it, you can do it if you want too!" Father was like "Well, okay. . . ." It just happened so fast. I didn't even know I would do such a thing.

Ironically, Mark did not get a scholarship for college because he graduated as a junior. He worked his way through college.

Future

Mark's plans for the future include giving back to his parents.

> Actually now that my father is becoming old. I want to, I have already planned as far as what am I going to do, and again, it's up to God if I can do that or not. A friend of mine said, "I'll graduate, I'll get a car, then I'll go do this, I'll do that, I'll do that." And I thought, "Well, fine, that's a good point too. You've got money, you do as it pleases you." But I think a little differently than that because my father is getting old now. I want to buy a house and then take care of my family that way. After my brother and sister are done with school and then through college and stuff, I would probably have my parents go back home, live there. Like for six months live over there, then come over here, then go back. That's how. That's what I'm planning to do.

Community

Mark and his family live in a subsidized apartment complex with a diverse population. Like others, his family tends to stay within their ethnic group. The management team has made efforts to provide services to the residents.

> We have a computer lab here. Sometimes I walk in there, I see black Americans, Hispanics, Asians, and all mixture of skin, very good. I see all these people staying there, learning, and doing their homework, which is very good. It is better for them to be there than to be on the streets, you know. And that would not have been done if the management team would not have provided that. So it's a very good situation.

Advice to New Immigrants

Asked what he learned from his experience and what kind of advice he would give to a child who had just arrived from another country, Mark answered that at first immigrants will likely feel the hardship of living in an unfamiliar culture with income inequalities. But he advises them to be persistent and work hard, and things will eventually improve.

LYNN

> By picking administration of justice, I knew that I could go into juvenile corrections and maybe make a difference, you know, in one person's life.

When I first interviewed her, Lynn was a nineteen-year-old woman living in Village View, a subsidized apartment complex in Virginia. Lynn is now a student in her third year at a nearby four-year university and is studying administration of justice.

Family Background

Lynn lives with her mother, brother, and sister. Lynn is the oldest sibling. Her sister is now seventeen and her brother is eleven. Her father does not live at home and Lynn did not volunteer information on him.

Lynn's mom is a foster parent, and children stay with the family for various periods of time. Lynn calls them her brothers and sisters; however, she explains that she manages not to get too attached to them.

> My mom is a foster parent also, so I have brothers and sisters coming and going all of the time. We've had some for five and a half years and some for like a couple weeks. She's had over 100 foster kids so it's like. . . . I have a lot. Only a few we keep in touch with and everybody says, "Oh, it's got to be so hard" and it's not. It's hard because you do get attached, but you know that when they come, you know, they are going to be there for a little while and then they are going to have to leave anyway, so you get attached, but not that attached so as where you can't leave them and they can't leave you.

She maintains contact with a few—those who stayed for a longer time.

> We get babies. She doesn't, she doesn't take them, the older ones, and she usually gets babies. And, in fact, I just talked to my brother and my

> sister—we had them for five and a half years. They had a birthday on Sunday and they turned thirteen. They were adopted so we just called them for their birthday and I talked to them.

Lynn has a very close relationship with her mother. When she was in high school and got a bad grade, the first thing she would do was to call her mother to let her know.

> There were days I would come home, "Oh I hate school, I hate it, I hate it, I hate it." My mom would be like, "What happened now?" And it was because I would have gotten, you know, a bad grade on a test or something. And if I had gotten a bad grade, I'm calling home before school ends, "Oh mom, I got a D on my test, I just wanted to call and let you know." And other than that I didn't, for school, school for me, it was like something I had to.

Living at Village View

Village View is a subsidized apartment complex that was previously run by a private management company. During that time, the property became known for high crime and drug dealing. Apartments were neglected and left in a state of disrepair. The county then took over the management of the property, with federal assistance provided by the Housing and Urban Development (HUD). Lynn arrived at Village View when she was three years old, during the previous property administration, and has been living there since.

Lynn says she does not mind living at Village View.

> I don't feel at a disadvantage here. This wasn't like a project or a ghetto or something; I never saw it like that. I mean, there were bad people around but it wasn't anything to, you know. I don't see it as a disadvantaged place at all.

Despite this affirmation, Lynn admits she was never allowed to play outside during the previous property management administration.

> Growing up I was always inside, I was never one to be outside. I was always inside and everything that I needed to do was done inside, I was always coming and going. Everything I wanted to do I did off of the property.

Friends

When she was in elementary school, Lynn had white friends for the most part.

> And the majority of my friends, when I was in elementary school were white . . . and they couldn't believe that I came from here after all of the negative stereotypes that they had heard, and everything.

When she entered intermediate school, Lynn met new people and started going to school with her cousin, with whom she remains friends to this day.

> I still have my best friend, my cousin. She goes to James Madison, so she's in Harrisonburg, so I don't get to talk to her that much. We e-mail each other a lot.

Even beyond elementary school, Lynn did not make friends with people at Village View. All her friends lived away from the property.

In high school, her two best friends were her cousin and another girl, whom Lynn and her cousin had known since eighth grade. Lynn recalls how, unbeknownst to her and her cousin, their friend became pregnant in high school.

> For the eleventh-grade year, she left. There were rumors, lots of rumors. People were coming up to me and my cousin and saying, "Your girl had a baby and you didn't know it." And I'm like "No, she didn't; no, she didn't. She would call me and tell me. She didn't tell me anything." We tried to call her a lot and we went to her house and got no response from her parents. Then one day I was going to get some glasses at the shopping center and I saw her mom's car and I said "There's her mom's car; she's here." And, my mom let me out of the car and when I went to where her mom's car was loading, there was a baby in the seat and I said, "Oh, whose baby?" And she's like, uh, I was like, "Is that your cousin's baby?" She's like "No." "Is it your mom's baby?" She's like, "No." And I was like, "Well, whose baby?" And she said, "You didn't hear?" I said "Hear what? You didn't tell anything!" And that's how I found out.

This story had a significant impact on Lynn. Beyond the fact that her friend did not trust her enough to share the news with her, Lynn is able to provide a very insightful analysis of her friend's situation.

> I don't think it was her choice to have a baby. I think that was just something that came along with what was going on in her life at the time. Her parents were going through a bitter divorce, you know. She wasn't being heard, she wasn't being listened to. The only person at that time that was listening to her was her boyfriend. He was an older guy. I kind of feel like he took advantage of a nice situation. He knew that she was vulnerable. He knew that she was having problems and he was needy also. So, they were two needy people together, and if you have two issues coming together you're going to create another issue.

Lynn has now reconnected with two old friends. The three young women had been accepted at different colleges, but decided after one year to transfer back to their local university.

> So now we're at Fairfield University, together again. We all transferred together. So now the three of us are always together. But I still keep in touch with my best friend from high school.

Lynn says she also likes to make friends with people older than she.

> And then there's another girl that, she's older, I usually have had older friends, and she's twenty-five. We're really close. She's taught me a lot.

Race Issues

Lynn is acutely aware of the stereotypes affecting African Americans in the community and is automatically suspicious of any judgment against Village View. For instance, the gathering of people outside apartments is not necessarily to be read as a sign of drug activity, but as a sign of community life.

> There were always people hanging out, you know, and as I got older I kind of liked to see that, you know, I thought "Okay, I know this person, that person" and you meet a lot of people. But being that it was a predominantly black neighborhood, it was made to look as though it was all drugs, and it was all bad, and it was, you know, stuff like that. But a lot of times, people fail to realize that here in Whitesville there's nothing, there's nothing to do.

In Lynn's view, racial inequality is definitely a daily reality and a no-win situation for black people.

> I mean, not to make it a racial thing, but . . . for the white kids and stuff they can go to the Town Square and hang out. We can't go to the Town

> Square and hang out because we're looked at as an eye-sore, and it's "You can't sit here in front of this door," and I've had that done to me before. You know, "You guys can't sit in front of this store, this person's business is being run away." And you know, stuff like that, so there's nothing to do. So, being that there were a lot of people here that had kids around the same age, more people tended to come here.

School Experience

Lynn makes it very clear that from the beginning, school was not her favorite place to be. She disliked the structured nature of school settings.

Most of her teachers in elementary and secondary schools were good, although some were less nurturing than others. Retrospectively, Lynn recognizes that the less nurturing teachers obtained better results with her than the more nurturing ones.

> In intermediate school, I had, I've had two or three black teachers in intermediate school. One of them, her name was Mrs. Smith, ooh, she was so mean to me. She was so mean. Yes. I would go into her class and it was me and a friend of mine named Amy. Both of us are black, and I was like, "She don't like black girls, she cannot stand us." And she would tell us, "Don't you come in my classroom smiling. Don't you, don't walk across the threshold of my door smiling." And, I saw her a couple weeks ago in church. I'd gone back to visit and I was like, "You know, you were really mean to me." And she was like "I knew you guys could get the work done. You were there to get the work done." And I had her for two years. But she kept us focused!

Lynn has a traumatic memory of the Virginia Literacy Passport test. She was able to pass reading in second grade, but math was a real weakness. She took the test over and over until she finally passed it in ninth grade, thanks to a very good teacher who worked with her after school. Lynn was placed in a class specifically designed to prepare for that test.

> But, when it came to the math part, the teacher, she really helped me. I missed it by three points, then I took it again and I missed it by two points. I was like, "Can't they give me the two points?" And I finally got it done and I was just so happy to get it over with.

She describes her high school experience as positive except when teachers and administrators reprimanded her for her attitude. Lynn explains that her "attitude" was a way of hiding her vulnerability. She was eligible for free lunch and did not want anyone to know it.

> All through high school I got free lunch and I, you know, I did all that stuff, and when I got all done I was like "I don't want anybody to know"—you know—it was, it was like trying to keep it away.

For the first few years of school, Lynn would often fake sickness, forcing her mother to pick her up. After a few times, her mother called a doctor who scared Lynn; she decided to stop faking.

Now in college, Lynn wishes she had worked harder and gotten better grades in high school.

> If I could do it all over again, I would. And I would make sure I had better grades. I would, you know, have prepared myself more.

Choice of Career

Lynn chose her major very deliberately. Seeing her friends and distant relatives dealing with the justice system and racial stereotypes, she decided to make a difference.

> I've always been one to say I'm very nosy, very nosy, and I always want to be in on everything and by picking administration of justice I knew that I could go into juvenile corrections and maybe make a difference, you know, in one person's life, maybe, you know, something like that. Otherwise, it's . . . always that I wanted to work with kids but I never wanted to be the teacher. I didn't want to be a teacher because I knew I'd wind up having to smack somebody [laughter] because I know how I was in school, the smart-mouth one, the one that is always, always has a comment, you know. Doesn't want to do the work and I always needed probing and pushing and I always needed that reassurance. I knew I didn't want to teach. I wanted to do something where I wasn't so confined to an office and I'd be able to get out in the field and see stuff and, you know, experience stuff. It's got to be able to keep me young; I don't want to ever get old.

Explaining Success and Failure

For Lynn, failing is more a matter of choice than conditions.

> Oh, my thing about that is, some people say, "Oh, well, it's peer pressure" you know, they're not able to do this, this, and that because their friends

> are telling them. . . well, I don't believe it. Everybody is given a choice, and you can choose to either do it or not do it, and I was just one who chose to do it, get it over with, and do something else. I didn't want to be someone that had to live here the rest of my life.

Lynn uses herself as an example.

> Because I could have been the bad one. I could have been the one not going to school. I could have been the one that, you know, decided, "Oh, I'm gonna have a baby," "Oh, I'm gonna do this and I'm gonna do that." But, it's just. . . . Why? I find no reason to, you know, I have better things to do. I knew that I wasn't dumb and I knew I wasn't, you know, going to have to sit here and do nothing. This isn't what it's all about. There's more to life than sitting at Village View and, you know, living and dying here. So, you know, the reason some people fail, maybe they do have problems, maybe they're not being properly tested and stuff, but otherwise, it's a crutch. They want to be hard. They want to be the one out there on the corner, you know, doing nothing.

Asked if her friend chose to have her baby, Lynn recognizes that it was not an active choice. Yet she finds it hard to feel sorry for her friend.

> So now, you know, in the situation that she's in, as she tells me, she'll call me at school and say, "I want to be living on campus. I don't want to be in the real world paying bills, and I. . . ." You know, and then, you reflect on that now, you know, but at the time when you were having your problems or whatever you weren't thinking rationally, I guess. Because she knew. I mean, she knew that she didn't have to have a baby at that time. If she had done what she needed to do, the baby would have been, you know, wouldn't be her issue.

MARY

> A child believes whatever it is told.

Family Background

When Mary was born in Bolivia in 1978, her mother was seventeen years old. Her father was not in Mary's life, and would not be for the longest time. She lived with her mother and her godmother. Mary comes from a large family; she has eight aunts and uncles, some of whom live in the U.S.

The family lived in poverty in Bolivia, although it was said that her grandfather once was wealthy and respected in the community. Alcoholism overcame him and he lost his wealth.

> My mother grew up with both her mother and father and my mom has stories about how her father was a very well-respected man and at one time he was rich. But after something happened with the political system in Bolivia and the business in which he was working in and his alcoholism, that the family lost that money and a lot of land. However, although it's been a fact in our family that maybe we came from a more privileged time a long time ago and it's all gone now.

Mary credits her family for being strong and caring, but she reserves her highest admiration and love for her mother.

When Mary speaks about her mother, her emotions come to the surface. She is intensely aware of her mother's sacrifice and she dreams of seeing her happy.

> My mom is a very extraordinary person. She didn't finish high school, she didn't go to college. She does say some things that she would like to see and I know she feels very limited and stuck in this life. She is a very spiritual person and she is very talented and she advises me on understanding others. It truly does pain me to think about my mom not realizing her goal, because of everything that she sacrificed for myself and my brother.

Even though alcoholism runs in Mary's family, her mother never gave in to it. Her Aunt Jane did, however, and Mary thinks that her cousin was affected by it. Mary observed that her aunt is to marry a very wealthy attorney with a beautiful house and a pool, yet she knows there is trauma in that part of the family.

From Bolivia to America

One day in November, mother and daughter embarked on a long journey. Mary remembers the exact date.

> I came to the United States when I was six years old—November 7, 1984. I remember very well. I wish to share another very truly personal thing with you. We came as illegal aliens to this country in 1984, and we crossed the border in Mexico. It was in a car ride, from one side to the

> other. We had someone help us get by. And all I remember is a plane ride. I remember the hotel room. I remember the sea as I looked down from the airplane—not fully understanding what was going on. I remember my mom asking me in Bolivia . . . she said, "Would you like to come with me or would you rather stay in Bolivia with your godmother?" And I remember telling her as a six-year-old frightened little child that "I will go wherever you go." I think I knew at that moment that my life had been decided and had taken a different turn.

At the time of her trip to the U.S., her mother was pregnant but Mary didn't know it yet.

They settled in a city on the East Coast where one of Mary's aunts, Jane, lived in an apartment. Mary has vivid memories of that initial cultural adjustment period. Despite her young age, she was keenly aware of a dramatic change in her life, in great part through the relationship she developed with her U.S.-born cousin, only three months older than Mary, and culturally very different.

> I had a cousin who is three months older than me, who was born here. And although we share a lot of things from our childhood, we are very much opposite. She grew up here—she is of an American culture. Her value system is American; my value system is based on Bolivian and that to me is being more collective, not individualistic; being more in-tuned with the people around you, and perhaps not so materialistic or future oriented. But also a sense of sadness of the past and of what's going on.

For Mary, the main differences between Bolivian and American dominant cultures are illustrated by the two sides of the family: those, like Mary and her mother, who had just arrived from Bolivia, who were more group oriented and less materialistic, and their hosts, who had been in the U.S. for a long time and were more materialistic, individualistic, and future-oriented.

Despite these dramatic adjustments to a new culture, Mary felt the protection and love of her mother. She did not feel deprived, although money was very tight. In comparison, her cousin had better access to material goods, but may have had a less rich spiritual and emotional life. Mary observed that her cousin did not go to college.

Only when she started school did Mary become aware of being economically disadvantaged. Being unable to go on special field trips or play sports and being on free lunch made her aware of it. She also realized that she was at a cultural and educational disadvantage. Her mother (not speaking English and not having completed high school) was not able to help her with schoolwork. Mary had to teach herself and learn on her own. She felt bitter about it, yet recognized that it helped her become independent faster.

Mary acquired a deep sense of competitiveness. She realized when she started school that the odds were against her, that her life was not a beautiful rose, and that she had to struggle. She observed through the study of the Civil Rights movement that oppressed people have to strive for something better. She knew she was not in an environment that supported her intellectually. She had responsibilities at home and took care of her younger brother, six years younger than Mary.

> I felt things against me. I wish I had had the money for tutors. I wish I had had an environment that supported me in that way. But I had other responsibilities at home, like taking care of my brother.

School Experience

Mary went to first grade in Bolivia, and then came to the United States. She remembers her first day in school.

> I remember a teacher, a big classroom, a lot of desks, and a lot of children. I went to first grade at Northeast Elementary School, and I do believe that was the only place that had ESL in my area.

She was kept in ESL for three years.

> By third grade, I became very upset that I was in ESL. I became more aware and conscious of what was going on. I didn't want to be in ESL and I wanted to learn a lot. I knew that in Bolivia I was five years old in first grade and I had learned a lot. I was writing, I was doing division, multiplication, a lot more than we did in the States. I got used to the system here and slacked off a lot.

Finally in fourth grade, by pure chance, she was placed in a normal English class instead of ESL. In fifth grade, she was placed in a lower-level math class.

> They tracked and I think that they placed me in the lower-level math and in the second class they moved me up to the regular math. And my best friend was in the upper-level math. And all the other smart people,

> children, were in the upper-level math. And it really, really bugged me. It really hurt me. I really wanted to be in the upper-level math. Maybe if I had gotten a tutor or said something about it, it would have happened.

Mary was a quiet girl who did not speak much. She was, therefore, quite surprised to hear that, when she was in fifth grade, someone had nominated her to run for president of the class.

> And she helped me out. But someone else won. I won for the class but not for the entire school. Then someone else moved and I became vice-president. I only remember attending one meeting and I had no clue as to what was going on. Absolutely no clue.

That same year, a gifted and talented program was established at her school. Mary was tested.

> But once again, I didn't understand the test. I remember that because I was feeling very frustrated. This was the first time where I think that I didn't even understand the directions to this test. I think that my frustration started there, in fifth grade. Because I slowly became more aware and conscious of what was going on.

With no one at home confident enough to question these practices, or even aware of what was happening, Mary started fending for herself. She became driven in high school, and quite popular. She was involved in many activities: drama, chorus show, Students against Drunk Driving, the Spanish Honor Society, and Junior Legislation.

Yet she was not fully satisfied with herself. She kept comparing herself to GT and AP-course students. Mary never was a 4.0 GPA/straight A student. She signed up for an AP class in American History but was extremely intimidated by her peers and the teacher, and missed class a lot. A missed school bus meant she couldn't get to school, and Mary often felt weak in her heart and spirit. She failed the class but was grateful for having had the opportunity to take on a challenge.

> I told my teacher I want to be in AP class, and she signed me up for the AP class, AP American History. And I failed that class. Of course I blamed myself for that, but even though I failed that class I was grateful to be in that class; even though that's the only F in my entire high school record. It was a way of me saying, "Well, this person is in GT and AP all their life, why not me? Why can't I be there? I want to learn. I'm here to

> learn." It was the reading and the writing and it was the intimidation—I felt very intimidated in that class by the teacher and the students.

She felt she had to constantly catch up with others, which led her to her sense of competitiveness.

> I became very goal-oriented. I was looking back through my papers and looking at all these goals I had written down and silly lists and that is proof positive of dreaming big. Things that I look back at now, it's like, "Really, you had that goal? Wow!" Like reading all of Shakespeare and I did begin on that quest. And, being a mountain climber or writing a book in Spanish. I still have some of these goals but the goals I had written down were huge.

This is the time when Mary experienced an eating disorder fairly common among teenage women: anorexia and bulimia. That year, Mary converted to a nondenominational church, where she found the discipline and sense of community across socioeconomic and ethnic lines that she had been looking for. She was baptized into that church within a week, and stayed involved for five years.

> It was during that year that someone from a nondenominational church approached me and I converted into this church, very rigid, very linear thinking. But in many ways, I found something that I didn't have before and that was a discipline, because my mom didn't raise us with discipline. It's not her fault. She was too preoccupied with other things. I was looking for things that other people my age weren't looking for, and I found that there, and I learned a lot of things from this church that I attended for about five years. This church really focused on making sure all of its members helped each other out. Its members were very devoted, Wednesday, Friday, Saturday, Sunday, Tuesday—they had things to do. Very positive. I had friends from different economic groups, different ethnic groups, different backgrounds, and that's what I value . . . having friends from different backgrounds. So it was that church also that . . . that in a way formed who I am now, but brought out that goal-oriented person and that brought out that striving person.

The church focused on converting a lot of people. Later (during her second year of college), she became increasingly frustrated with its main goal of recruiting new members, its rigidity, and decided to leave it. She then realized that all the friends she had made through the church discontinued their relationships with her.

Mary won a full four-year scholarship to college through the Early Identification Program. Through this program, she was one of sixty students in her geographical area to win this scholarship. When she graduated from high school, it struck her that this graduation was for her mom as well as for herself. She had fulfilled her mom's dream to see her children go to college. Mary felt the responsibility and joy that came with this insight, though she recognized that too much of it is bad. Her college experience has been an enactment of the American Dream story, thanks to the full scholarship.

Interracial Couple

Mary is engaged to an African American man she met in college. This relationship was a turning point in her life: first, because in her family, men are not perceived as a strong and positive presence, and she had to learn to accept that a man can be such; second, because her involvement with an African American man initially caused a strong negative reaction from her mother. She has learned a lot about the African American culture and what she calls "code switching."

> Through our relationship, I have learned many things about myself and the American culture. Because we are an interracial couple, we are both interested in intercultural relations, sociology, and even international affairs. We are always talking about issues of this sort.

From America to Bolivia

Mary made the journey back to Bolivia during her first year in college.

> I went after my first semester in college. I went back and I went to see my father. However, that experience wasn't positive. Not at all. It was very positive in the sense of my maturity and understanding my cultural roots and my family; but with my relationship with my father, it was not. And I'm very understanding of that situation and grateful for what I have because my mom was everything I needed. I made sure he understood from me that I would be here to keep in contact with him and that once I did my part of keeping contact with him once, he had to reply. If he didn't reply, then there was no reason for a relationship there. So, there is no relationship. None whatsoever.

However, Mary does feel strong roots to Bolivia. One of her majors is Spanish.

> I took it upon myself to make sure that I kept on learning Spanish. Actually, I would not consider myself a person that has English as a skill; I struggle with writing English. I sometimes stop whenever someone is speaking to me in English and wish that were Spanish. Although I know I speak more English, and it actually comes more fluid and I think in English, Spanish speaks to my heart and I feel more at ease. I feel at home. That's why I have taken Spanish classes from eighth grade on. And that's another internal dilemma, very small, but nevertheless it is one. I do live with my boyfriend, and we only speak English unless we are practicing little words in Spanish. And, I would really love to hear Spanish in my house. And that's why I can't wait until he learns more Spanish.

Beyond the moving and inspiring individual stories, some patterns and common features emerged across the cases, describing and explaining the process of resilience. Let us now examine these patterns in the following chapters.

• 3 •

Barriers to Success and Their Effects on Students at Risk

Witnessing the drama and sometimes tragedy that surround children growing up in poverty, one may feel powerless and indignant. Yet hidden behind the stories are the seeds of a deeper understanding of the process of resilience in students at risk, and with it the key to what would close the achievement gap along social class lines. I conducted a cross-case analysis of the seven stories, which led to the discovery of a complex process, and a possible path leading from adversity to success. In this chapter, we will examine which barriers children of poverty encountered along the way and how these barriers affected them.

ADVERSITY

Adversity takes on different faces, as we have seen through these life stories. No less than nine can be identified and will be examined individually.

- Poverty
- Racial and ethnic identity
- Isolation and lack of exposure
- Hostile environments
- Lack of educational history: learning how to learn
- Linguistic and cultural adjustment
- Conflict between school and home
- Neglect and abuse
- Additional barriers

Poverty

All respondents belonged to low-income families or environments. Therefore, it is not surprising to see poverty emerge as a salient issue in almost all interviews. What is less expected, however, is how some of the participants felt labeled and stigmatized by their lower social-class status, and their subsequent reaction to it. It is also somewhat surprising that, in Ray's case, the issue of poverty did not appear to be significant.

Lynn resented being on free lunch in school because it identified her as disadvantaged. "I thought, 'I don't want anybody to know,' I was trying to keep it away."

Renée became aware of her social class status only after her father left home and they moved to the ghetto area of a midwestern city. "We moved to the inner city, into the low-income housing project. And, that's when it first hit me that we didn't have money." She, too, resented being on free lunch at school, because it identified her as poor, and other kids would make fun of her.

> The kids that didn't get free lunch usually packed their lunch; so anybody who had the little government lunch were easily identified. It was always embarrassing.

For Vince, whose parents were sharecroppers in rural Mississippi, there was an early awareness of poverty. At a young age, Vince observed that there were not enough resources to provide for all their needs, and that he and his brothers were expected to work on the farm to help out, even when school was in session.

> [In the '60s] the split sessions stopped. And, the people were required to go to school in September. The farmers just could not afford to allow their children to do so. Had to keep them out, to do the harvesting. And, I remember missing, oh, anywhere from two and a half months—September, October, most of November. Sometime it was after Thanksgiving before we went to school. And that meant you missed three of the eight months. So, uh, because you're harvesting. And there was no provision to catch up on anything.

For Vince, therefore, one of the stigmas associated with poverty was to be denied proper schooling. Yet at the same time, he is quick to say that he never went hungry and never went out with dirty clothes. Indeed, there was a certain dignity associated with poverty, and certainly no sense of shame or embarrassment about it.

> Although we had limited dollars, I don't ever remember going hungry. I'm sure I didn't get what I wanted to eat all the time . . . but I don't remember going hungry, you know. Sure we were limited in terms of educational opportunities, but we did get into school every year and were supported very strongly by our parents in there.

For Lori (as for Vince), poverty was certainly limiting yet not leading to trauma, in part because no one was really wealthy where she lived. Growing up, she did not see a gap between wealthy and poor—everyone was struggling.

For Lori, poverty and her parent's lack of education translated into an educational deficit, which she found difficult to eliminate. Her children were as sophisticated in fourth grade as she was when she finished college, but poverty also gave her a survivor's mentality, which she considers a positive thing.

Even though Mary lived in just one room with her mother and brother, she did not feel the impact of poverty until she started school.

> I wish I had had the money for tutors. I wish I had an environment that supported me in that way.

Instead, she had additional responsibilities, such as taking care of her brother while her mother was at work, or taking care of her mother who did not feel confident enough in her ability to speak and understand English and used Mary as a translator.

Poverty did not appear to be a salient issue for Mark and Ray. Mark grew up in Pakistan, where his father had his own business selling medical instruments to doctors and hospitals; his mother did not work. When they came to the United States, his father took on a job as a dispatcher at an airport and his mother does not work outside the home. Mark and his family live in a subsidized apartment complex, yet the only reference Mark made about poverty is when he dreams about the future. Upon graduation from the university, he wants to provide for his parents so his father will no longer have to work.

Mark is not the first person in his family to receive a post-secondary education. His grandmother was a doctor and both his parents went to college in Pakistan. Thus, Mark's poverty is perhaps more associated with immigration than with a long-standing low-income history.

Ray, isolated from the rest of society, was a resident in an institution for people with mental disabilities. All residents came from lower socioeconomic classes; therefore, understandably for him, poverty did not have any special meaning.

Poverty appears to have the following properties for most respondents:

It distracts from school time and schoolwork. Even those respondents who were not paid for their work had to perform different types of duties that took time away from studying. Lori had the duties of a full-time homemaker, and she also had a job when she was in high school. Renée had to baby-sit, clean the house, and even sell products door-to-door on a routine basis. Vince had to work on the farm and help in the house. Mark did not have to work until he was in college because his parents wanted him to concentrate on school, but Mark's parents, as we have seen, were college-educated and placed a high value on education. Lynn did not have a job but helped her mother with foster care.

It takes on a new dimension in rural settings. In addition to the many facets of urban poverty, rural poverty conveys or reinforces a sense of isolation and remoteness. Both Lori and Vince comment on this.

It is compounded by racial segregation. Asked if poverty was worse than segregation, Vince established a direct link between racial segregation and poverty.

> I mean they were linked. Very, very linked. I mean, the segregation and what had happened historically, you know, caused in a large part poverty. The struggles, however, in terms of having access to things, you know, was I think probably even more pronounced with poverty.

It restricts social life. Ray's social life was the most restricted because of the quasi-military institutional environment where he lived. It was so restrictive that he was not able to adjust to a home situation during the holidays, and the relatives who had offered to take him home for a week had to take him back to City Home. Vince's social life was reduced to very few activities: basketball at school, meeting friends, and church on Sundays.

Lori's social life was nonexistent because she was so isolated—even from her high school—that unless a friend would come and pick her up to go to a game, she wouldn't have been able to go.

> I was a good student, and I'd have to speak at the PTA or I'd go to something and my friend lived twenty miles on the other side of town, out in the country. Her mother was a schoolteacher and her dad was a carpenter, so they were actually far better off than we were. And they used to drive the forty miles or whatever to pick me up and take me to stuff. Because my mom really couldn't afford the gas to do it.

Most of all, poverty seems to translate into a lack of power, a state of mind where one physically and mentally feels restricted. The metaphor of confinement and restriction often appears in the respondents' language and is explorer further later in the chapter.

Racial and Ethnic Identity

This category refers to the specific experience of adversity for nonwhites due to the color of their skin or their ethnic background. All nonwhite respondents experienced their "nonwhiteness" as a topic of discussion.

Having grown up in the Deep South when racial segregation was a deep-rooted legal and cultural social system, Vince was most affected by this form of hardship. He witnessed the Civil Rights movement and the desegregation of schools and other public facilities. He also witnessed the backlash created by the newly acquired civil rights.

> The Civil Rights Act of 1964 really outlawed discrimination in public accommodation but it didn't take place in a lot of the small towns until long after that. The public accommodation thing took a long time to get around to. You read about the lynching and you also knew that there were a lot of them that took place that you didn't read about—because it didn't make the paper—that was very frightening. And that raised a tremendous amount of anxiety, I mean, crops were burning and those kinds of things were very, very common.

Although racial discrimination became outlawed, in reality it did not cease to exist. Born three decades later, Lynn observed that racial discrimination is alive and well.

> We can't go to the Town Square and hang out because we're looked at as an eyesore, and it's "You can't sit here in front of this door" and I've had that done to me before. You know, "You guys can't sit in front of this store, this person's business is being run away."

Ray remarked that residents were segregated at City Home. There were white pavilions and black pavilions. Beyond that, he only alluded to racial discrimination in an oblique way, perhaps alluding to fights that may have occurred between blacks and whites.

> Yes, they had, they had a few . . . whites had one cottage, blacks had a few cottages. It was, yes, they had a lot of . . . but see I didn't really get

> to see a lot of it because I was in Poplar. So, we didn't get to see the whole, but we knew it was. Where you may have staff taking up for a white child, or staff may not take up for the black child because he shouldn't be doing it anyway. You know, it's just that a lot of that was, a lot of abuse, a lot of stuff that was covered up.

Mark, who was born in Pakistan and arrived in the U.S. in 1990, did not mention suffering because of his ethnic background; however, he tended to socialize with non-Americans (black and white) only, especially in high school. Mark did not seem to have been adversely affected by the color of his skin, in the way that African Americans were.

Mary, who was born in Bolivia in 1978, did not seem to experience adversity directly due to her ethnic background either. However, when she mentioned being intimidated by AP teachers and students (a class she eventually failed), one wonders whether the cause of this anxiety might have been related to a cultural divide.

As for Lori and Renée, the only whites in the group, they became cognizant of race as a social issue. Lori first experienced a rift with her family in a discussion about racial segregation, and Renée became aware of her socioeconomic status when her family moved into an all-black neighborhood.

Race and ethnic background seem to play an important role in the way individuals perceive themselves as mirrored by society at large. If being white is perceived as the norm, anyone nonwhite will at least carry an awareness of his/her difference—an awareness that can become a heavy burden, especially when combined with poverty.

Isolation and Lack of Exposure

A third form of adversity for the respondents consisted in the form of isolation and lack of exposure to educational and cultural opportunities. For Vince, harvesting time was particularly harsh in that respect, since he was denied the opportunity to attend school, sometimes for up to four months. But the system of racial segregation also isolated an entire group (African Americans) from the rest of society, and denied them the opportunities that were available to whites. Vince never had an opportunity to play football because it simply was not offered in black schools then. Even though he was interested in economics, his undergraduate university "had very limited resources in economic studies."

Lori grew up in a remote place in the mountains where no amenities were available. Lori never saw bananas or other fruits; when her hosts' house burned down, they had to watch helplessly, as there was no fire station in her county. Living twenty miles away from school, she had no transportation to participate in special activities. Her visual impairment also left her feeling isolated from her surroundings. "I felt in the dark," she confessed. Access to books was nonexistent until she started school. Later, in high school, she was never challenged with difficult courses.

Renée endured a living hell that she could not share with anyone, so afraid of possible consequences that she lied about her mother's abuse. The silence she was condemned to observe isolated her from her peers, teachers, and those who could have helped her. In junior high and high school, Renée was never given the challenge of advanced courses.

Mark was immediately placed in an ESL class that did not allow him to socialize with other students. Although his uncle took good care of him, he suffered a sense of isolation from being away from home. His social life was limited to a few friends at school.

Ray suffered most from a sense of isolation and lost opportunities, being physically confined to an institution. This confinement mirrored the mental and developmental confinement he felt due to his retardation label.

Mary's sense of isolation and lack of exposure to opportunity manifested itself in cultural alienation, an acute awareness that she was sensitive to others in a culture where individualism is praised, and that her aspirations were spiritual in a culture where materialism and consumerism are highly valued. She sensed early on that she had to catch up with her peers, and became obsessively goal-oriented. For example, in a manner strikingly similar to Richard Rodriguez, Mary gave herself the goal of reading all of Shakespeare's writings in one year.

As for Lynn, even though she initially denied it, Village View represented both her lack of opportunities and the place in which she was stuck.

> I didn't want to be someone that had to live here the rest of my life. I want to be out of here. I don't, this isn't what I wanted, you know, this isn't what my life's going to be. I don't want to live here. I don't want to raise my kids here. If I had my way, I wouldn't be here now.

As a result of their childhood isolation, respondents had to struggle later when they reached undergraduate or graduate school. They all had to play "catch-up" when confronted with their more privileged peers. Even Ray, who did not reach an advanced level of schooling, wishes he had been given more intellectual challenges. Asked what he thought was the biggest obstacle he had experienced, he answered:

> I think it was not being given the chance to really get a good education.

Hostile Environments

This category refers to the social institutions and environments in which the lives of our respondents unfolded. Family and school, as well as social, political, and cultural climates, represented—in different ways—obstacles in the lives of the respondents.

Vince grew up in the South at the end of the racial segregation era. This had a significant impact on his life. It meant that his rights as an individual were curtailed by a set of rules that permeated virtually all aspects of his young life: school, life on the farm, the way he spent his weekends, the sports he played, the friends he could have, the church he could attend, even his self-concept.

Then the Civil Rights movement brought new "hope and fear" into his life. He discovered hope in the form of higher aspirations for himself and his entire race, but also fear caused by white supremacists' retaliation.

> Random acts of violence, violations of people's civil liberties were very commonplace.

Vince was also affected by late mechanization on the farm combined with a change in the unfolding of the school year, which severely limited his access to education.

> Mechanization in agriculture did not take place in Mississippi until the late '70s. So we really did not experience a significant opportunity of mechanization while we were growing up, so that meant labor was very important and hit some of the larger families. . . . We had in school what we called 'split session' at one time. There was a summer session of school that went for about a month and a half or so, and therefore school did not start in the fall again until about November. That changed toward the early part of the '60s. The split sessions stopped. And the people were required to go to school in September. The farmers just could not afford to allow their children to do so.

Lori lived a remote and isolated environment. The mountains of Georgia offered little awareness of the changes that were taking place in the

'50s and early '60s. This closed environment did not shield her from the humiliation of being poor and underprepared for school. Lori stated that there were no haves and have-nots in her community, yet she felt smaller, less developed, and had lower self-esteem than most of her peers. Her lack of knowledge about racial segregation led her to be rejected by a black girl in Atlanta with whom she had wanted to strike up a conversation.

Also noteworthy in Lori's story is the impact of the social context on her physical and psychological health in terms of lack of medical care facilities and health insurance coverage.

> You never went in for any kind of preventive health care. If you were very sick, you went to the doctor's. I had a lot of illnesses when I was young. I had pneumonia, I had chronic bronchitis, and chronic throat infections and ear infections until I was about thirteen.

Lori's family environment also played a role in the adversity she experienced as a child. After her parents divorced, Lori endured a period of homelessness and vagrancy. When her mother started working at the local factory, Lori became the caretaker of the house. Tension between her stepfather and the children increased as time went by.

Lori was always a good student, so even though the first day in school came as a shock to her—as she realized how little she knew—and the early years were sometimes a struggle, eventually Lori came to see school as a very positive environment.

With her mother, Mary came to this country illegally and at a great risk to both their lives, at a time when policymakers were determined to check the flow of immigrants, especially those coming from Central and South America. Even though Mary may have been too young to understand the meaning of her flight to America, she clearly came to realize its implications retrospectively, and recalled it as one of the most significant events in her life. Because her immigration was illegal, she grew up in a social context in which she was not welcome, and her clandestine status caused additional stress.

A new immigrant in the same time period, Mark grew up in a similar context, although he did not mention whether or not he first came to the U.S. as a legal immigrant. Upon arrival, Mark and Mary both stayed with close relatives who had been living in the U.S. for a long time. Staying with uncles and aunts seemed to have facilitated the acculturation process in an environment that was totally new and not particularly kind to recent immigrants.

Mark also suffered from his family's absence during the first two years of his life in the United States and cites that as the greatest obstacle he faced at that time.

Ray lived in a city-run institution for mentally disabled children and adults at a time when our understanding of disability was virtually nonexistent. Later, in the aftermath of the Civil Rights movement, many private citizens and groups organized themselves to sensitize the general population to the plight of the disabled. One of these organizations was the Special Olympics, which may very well have saved Ray's life, and certainly saved his spirit. Until that time, though, Ray lived in a social environment that more resembled a laboratory than a community.

In that setting, Hemlock represented the ultimate hostile environment. Hemlock was a jail inside the institution, a place where residents who misbehaved were sent for a few days.

> You'd get two meals a day. All you had was a green mattress. There was not even a toilet in there. It was just like being incarcerated. And that was for like three days to a week.

In a milder way, any academic setting represented a hostile environment for Ray, in that they made him feel inadequate and unwelcome.

Lynn's story tells of the persistence of racial hostility against African Americans, especially poor ones, decades after the Civil Rights Act, which gave Vince hope and fear. Racial tension in the late '80s and early '90s followed an upward curve that surprised many. Riots in large cities following stories of police abuse or what was perceived as injustice against blacks brought home the seriousness of racial relations in America today. Lynn's testimony reveals this theme of racial tension and explains the defensiveness I perceived in her when we first met. Facing Lynn, I became aware of my whiteness and the advantageous position in which I was cast as the one asking the questions. This tension dissolved in subsequent exchanges through electronic mail.

Renée grew up in the '70s, a decade marked by profound social changes in America, a growing gap between the younger and older generations, the increasing opposition to the Vietnam war, the Watergate scandal and Nixon's resignation from the White House, and changing perceptions of the role of the United States in the world. Her father's absence and later her parents' divorce left her vulnerable to her mother's physical abuse.

Until she reached her junior year in high school, Renée experienced school as a hostile environment. "Kids made fun of me," she reported, and teachers ignored her. Because of her family situation, Renée never asked for the support she might have received from teachers and/or administrators. Home diminished the influence school might have had, and school was no relief to Renée, and sometimes even added insult to injury by making her feel inadequate. As a result, she missed school regularly, took little interest in what was being taught, and made herself almost invisible.

Lack of Educational Tradition: The Difficulty of Learning How to Learn

This category represents a form of adversity perhaps more specific to low-income, working-class individuals than any other category (excluding poverty). It refers to the challenge of having no help with schoolwork, no culture of education, no tools for studying, and, in some cases, no value placed on education in the home environment. This lack of environmental support has long been identified as a condition that perpetuates the achievement gap between privileged and underprivileged students.

In all but one case (Mark, whose parents had a college education in Pakistan), participants in the study were first-generation achievers in their families. In some cases, parents valued education and encouraged their children to pursue learning habits. In others, parents were indifferent to education and discouraged their children from applying themselves to schoolwork. In most cases, they had to find their own learning opportunities.

In Vince's family, the first to graduate from high school and go to college was his fourth brother. Vince's parents could read and write, but did not have a high school education. Thus, they were only able to help Vince and his brothers in the early stages of their schooling. Two of Vince's older brothers did not graduate from high school; instead they married and took jobs.

Moreover, as observed earlier, Vince consistently missed a good part of the first semester of school throughout his elementary and high school education. The quality of his teachers did not quite make up for what he missed and he later suffered a significant setback.

> I know, until this day, and I experienced it in graduate school also, the lack of exposure, the lack of acquiring some basics—and I have limits today on basics and one of the reasons for it is the access, particularly at the elementary and early-on levels. I suffered from that in graduate school and have constraints, you know, even today. I had to study five times more than the folks that were around me. They just sort of got it. And I sort of had to work at it.

Renée's parents did not go to college.

> My dad graduated from high school; my mother did not. She went through eleventh grade. I believe people just pushed her through. I don't think she learned anything.

When living with her mother, Renée routinely missed school because her mother had work plans for her that day. School was not a positive environment for Renée. In addition, Renée's mother did not allow her to do homework at home. Renée literally had to "sneak in" homework and make sure that her mother did not catch her studying. For Renée, then, homework represented the potential threat of being beaten, a consequence she understandably tried to avoid at all cost. She would hastily work on her assignments right before classes.

> So I'd sit there trying to get it done in the hallway. And I did have a study hall and I'd try to do some in study hall too. But it's still, it's hard if you don't do homework at home.

In tenth grade, when she went to live with her father, it actually came as a surprise to her that he encouraged her to do homework.

> When I moved in with my dad, he started working with me. He said, you know, "You need to do your homework." And I thought, "What do you mean I need to do my homework?" He said, "You need to sit at the table and do homework." I said, "Why?" You know, I just thought that was weird. I said, "Shouldn't I do it in study hall?" He answered, "No, you do it at home. You go over the stuff . . ." you know, and he would just work with me.

In college, she experienced her first setback when one of her professors gave her a D and refused to convert it to a C in exchange for extra work. While this grade caused her to graduate without honors, it helped her realize that she needed to apply herself to her studies if she wanted to graduate.

Mary's mother did not graduate from high school, and was not in a position to help Mary due to her lack of English language skills. Thus, Mary had to chart her own course. She noticed that during her years in elementary schools, she was placed in lower-level classes even though she wanted to be in higher-track courses. It was difficult for her to speak up, and her mother did not know how to demand a change.

> And nobody in my family understood what was going on. They just knew that I was doing well in school, but they didn't know that there were all these other things.

Later, Mary assumed a parental role with her younger brother as he entered school and was able to help him avoid this type of situation.

Mark was the only participant whose parents had a college education. They encouraged him to devote most of his time to studying and, unlike most high school students, he did not work until he started college.

It is hard to know what educational tradition existed in Ray's family, since he was abandoned. In his case, the institution acted as the family environment. Ray's testimony tells the story of a regimented set of activities designed to keep a sense of control and quasi-military discipline, rather than to promote the pleasure of studying. Ray was not considered disciplined enough to get an education, so they kept him inside, and by doing so they denied him the opportunity to educate himself—a no-win situation for him.

> They had some residents who went outside of the institution for education. They thought that I wasn't at that level of being outside of the institution. I needed to be supervised.

Eventually, Ray was sent to a regular school and placed in special education classes. He loved being with other students, although his coresidents seemed embarrassed to show where they were from, hiding at the back of the school bus on their way back to the institution. When he left City Home, Ray read on a third-grade level. He is currently taking evening classes through the Kennedy Institute and is now reading at the fourth-grade level. His goal to eventually graduate at the twelfth-grade level is an enormous challenge but the Kennedy Institute, which also sponsors the Special Olympics, provides the environment that Ray needs.

Through his son's education, Ray experiences what happens in a mainstream school. Unable to assist his son with content, Ray still provides leadership and encouragement. The first time I called his house to discuss the possibility of an interview, I was put on hold for a good ten minutes. Ray eventually picked up the phone and, after apologizing, explained that he had had a discussion with his son, who had not kept up his grades lately.

Lori grew up in a family with very little education. Her father had the highest educational level (high school diploma), but she did not live with him or his side of the family. Her mother and her stepfather had an elementary school education. With the exception of a Bible and a hymnal, there were no books in her house. As soon as she started school, she felt the effect of the sterile environment in which she had been raised.

On her first day of school, she realized she was far behind her peers in school readiness. This made her very angry with her mother for not having prepared her. Lori's first years in school were an attempt to keep her head above the water. Even though she was a bright student, her self-esteem was very low, due in part to her lack of readiness, and in part to an ever-moving "home."

High school was another big adjustment. It is ironic that a student like Lori, who academically did very well, had such a negative social experience in school, because of her perceived lack of physical and social qualities. Somehow, places of learning become so socially normative that they make some students feel like outsiders.

When she reached post-secondary education, Lori again struggled with the deficit left by her lack of exposure to educational and cultural opportunities. She felt behind in many areas and had to study harder than others to simply catch up, an activity from which she will never feel free.

Lynn also suffered from a lack of education, even though she did not specifically identify it that way. One of her most challenging episodes in school had to do with the math portion of the state Literacy Passport test. It took her three attempts to finally pass the test, despite help from her teachers.

From the beginning, school was a painful experience for Lynn. She said she hated sitting down, listening, and studying. She did not want to be in school, and she even tried to fake being sick. Expressing such strong feelings of opposition to school environment can be seen as a sign of culture shock not unlike feelings expressed by travelers when they first arrive in a foreign culture.

Linguistic and Cultural Adjustment

This category refers to the difficulty two respondents experienced when they were born in a different country and immigrated to the United States. Mark was eleven and Mary was six when they arrived. The first few years of their life in this country were marked with the challenge of learning a new language, adapting to a new culture, finding their identity in it, understanding new values, and deciding what role they would play.

Mark had the added difficulty of being separated from his parents and siblings during those two crucial years. He lived with his uncle who treated him like a son, yet some of his remarks point to the trauma of being uprooted without the support of his parents around.

Mary was smuggled into the U.S. with her mother. She remembers the different sequences of the trip, but it is difficult to say for sure that she had an awareness of changing places and traveling to a country where she was not welcome.

The struggle Mary and Mark experienced was to reconcile two cultures with sometimes conflicting values. Mark seemed to have been less torn than Mary over this issue, immediately seeking to please his teachers and avoiding conflict with peers at all cost. Mary, however, struggled for a long time to adjust to her new cultural environment. She felt different from her American-raised cousin, and was angry when schools placed her in lower-track courses. In high school, she became obsessively goal- and future-oriented, a feature that she associated with American culture. Once in college, she started reestablishing a connection to Bolivia and Hispanic people. She values cultural diversity and hopes to have a career in that field.

Conflict between School and Home

Virtually all respondents experienced conflict between school and other parts of their lives. Work, stress, and vital concerns competed with school for the participants' attention and commitment.

As indicated earlier, work was an important part of Vince and Lori's daily lives, and used up much of their energy.

Stress caused by linguistic and cultural adjustment was a salient category in the lives of Mary and Mark, and to a certain extent, Lynn.

Ray and Renée were dealing with abuse and its related issues, such as psychological trauma, secrecy, isolation, and the energy it takes to simply survive, day-in and day-out. Ray's label of mental retardation influenced the way school viewed him and, in return, how he viewed it.

Neglect and Abuse

This category refers to the physical and emotional torture some respondents endured during their childhood and youth. For Renée and Ray, this was the most salient issue in their lives, more important than any other. Neglect and abuse occur in all socioeconomic backgrounds and all ethnic groups. In the cases of Renée and Ray, however, neglect and abuse occurred in the context of poverty, and their stories demonstrate the effect of this particular facet of adversity in a working-class context. Some of the effects of adversity will be analyzed in the next section.

Renée and Ray's experiences reminded me of Victor Frankl's account of his life in concentration camps. Physical abuse is often not included in research on adversity and resilience, yet this particular form of trauma cannot be ignored, since it is—sadly—part of the human experience. Renée and Ray survived physical abuse as others survived racial segregation and prejudice, and their stories not only deserve to be told, but to educate us on the process of resilience.

In Ray's case, physical abuse was perpetrated most often by staff, but also at times by other residents. It was arbitrary, but Ray was one of 300 in his pavilion and therefore had one chance in 300 to be beaten. Ray's life was similar to what one might experience in a prison. Renée's form of abuse was more personalized—she was one of only three who could get beaten on any day. Her environment was less regimented and more chaotic. On some days, her mother used her as a confidante, on others as a victim.

Both cases confirm Frankl's discovery that nothing can break an indomitable human spirit. Both respondents overcame physical and psychological abuse through an understanding that transcended the physical and the tangible. Although the experiences diminished some of their capacities, both were extremely upbeat, accommodating, and surprisingly trusting.

Additional Barriers

Lori was legally blind but did not know it until she started school. Lynn and Mary grew up without their fathers. Renée had severe scoliosis that necessitated major back surgery in the summer preceding her junior year in high school. All these can be seen as additional barriers, which intensify the effects other barriers have on students at risk.

EFFECTS OF ADVERSITY

What effects did all these obstacles have on the respondents? Let us examine the different ways participants were affected by and responded to these different forms of hardship. The analysis of the participants' stories yielded six categories describing the effects these obstacles had on them.

- Fear and anxiety
- Resentment

- Internalization
- Shame
- Early maturity
- Self-protection

Fear and Anxiety

Referring to the Civil Rights movement and its effects on African American people, including himself, Vince talks about "hope and fear." It is important to note that fear was not a result of adversity, but of the retaliation against the Civil Rights movement: the unreported violence he witnessed, especially in the South. The fear refers to what one feels in a climate of social injustice when authorities show indifference to or even perpetrate violence against one class of people. Vince accurately read the threatening symbol represented by the burning cross in his churchyard.

Even though her community was rather small and with few differences in socioeconomic status, Lori often felt anxious in school because she felt different, smaller, less sophisticated, less prepared than others. Yet she was clearly one of the best students in school. Her teachers knew she was capable of excelling academically, but her low self-esteem impaired her self-confidence as strongly as her blindness impaired her vision. To this day, when Lori works with people in need, she stresses the importance of self-esteem by establishing meaningful relationships with them.

In the institution where he was a resident, Ray lived in constant fear of the unpredictable: an unjust punishment, a staff member's arbitrary decision, a violent resident, fights, his enemies, and even death (if it happened to his sister, it could also happen to him). Later, when he discovered the Special Olympics group and spent his weekends out playing, he described feeling anxious when returning to the institution on Sunday evening.

Renée spent the first fifteen years of her life in fear of her mother. School was also a fearful experience, although not as much so as life at home. She described herself as a shy, compliant student, often ridiculed by other students and ignored by her teachers. Her fear caused her to have very few friends and to confide in no one, accentuating the sense of isolation in which she lived.

Mary experienced the anxiety we all feel when we are outside our element. Her acute sensitivity increased her awareness of being different, of being in another culture with different values. In Mary's case, anxiety translated into behaviors such as anorexia and bulimia. In high school, she was often absent because of anxiety.

Fear and anxiety inhibit social skills, an important component in human development, and certainly a valued quality in American society. Fear and anxiety also inhibit study habits, curiosity, and ease of expression that lead to achievement in school.

Resentment

Along with fear and anxiety often came resentment as a result of adversity. This anger was provoked by a sense of injustice and the lack of power to annihilate this injustice.

In his own words, Vince, who grew up in a segregated community, became very bitter and threatened by a system that considered him inferior solely because of the color of his skin.

Lori felt resentment against her mother for keeping her in ignorance and not preparing her for school. Lori and her siblings also felt resentment against their stepfather who did not do much around the house.

Until Renée was out of danger, she did not realize how much anger she suppressed against her mother. When she decided she wanted to go to college and realized her grades might not allow her to do so, she felt resentment.

> And then I got so afraid I wasn't going to get into college because of my ACT scores and I got all bitter towards her again. I was just thinking, you know, if she would have encouraged me to do homework, if she would have helped me in school or helped me to do homework, if she would have told me to take the right classes, then I wouldn't be in this situation. And I got really mad at her again.

Lynn expressed her resentment against authority by expressing a dislike for the structured nature of school, but her anger sounded more like a cry against the injustice of being poor and African American in a society that devalued those two characteristics.

> I had positive experiences in high school, except for times when people would tell me that I had an attitude and that I would never get anywhere with the attitude that I had and stuff like that.

Mary's resentment turned inward when she was in high school.

> When I was a sophomore in high school, I became obsessed with being thin, that disease that plagues many teenagers, bulimia and anorexia. I struggled with it for a relatively short time, but it did affect my health.

Internalization

To different degrees, all respondents internalized the image that was projected upon them through adversity. That is, they all became convinced that they were not capable of beating the odds against them. Some admit that to this day they still struggle with this subconscious psychological process.

Vince internalized the message that society sent him—the notion that he was inferior because of his race—even as he knew cognitively that this was not true. Speaking of racial segregation, Vince said:

> You felt very threatened, you felt bitter about it. And I have to say, you also felt inferior. There is—I don't care how much you fight it—an inferiority complex that develops around it. And it's very difficult to fight it off. And subconsciously, it's going to be there. You know, very few people are able to fight it off in a conscious and a subconscious way.

Speaking about the problem with her stepfather, who had no employment and did not help around the house, Lori acquired the notion that the problem was not with him, but with the rest of the household. This belief spread to the stigmatization of herself and her immediate relatives (her mother and siblings).

> I think because my mother's family spent so much time telling us how lucky we were to have somebody, kind of made me feel like there must be something wrong with us, nobody wants us.

Renée knew her abusive mother was not to be trusted, yet she came to believe the messages that her mother communicated to her:

> While living with my mother, I considered myself a worthless nobody. She constantly beat me and called me obscene names. She always told me I was of no importance to anyone. I believed it and developed a very low self-image.

As a resident in a less-than-reputable institution, Ray (like many others) was treated more as a prisoner than a patient. As a result, he also behaved like a prisoner.

> I was wild at that time, you know, hyper. . . . I had to fight sometimes. I had to stand for what I believed was right. I lost a couple matches, but I won . . . . But I was on punishment every time, that's why I say . . . no matter if you win or lose, you still gonna get punished.

To a lesser extent, Mark also struggled with internalization as a new immigrant from Pakistan.

> In the beginning, yes it was hard. I didn't really know what was going on, how to behave, how to act, so I would look similar to other people.

Lynn was a junior in college, doing very well academically, yet she hated school from the beginning.

> I hated school. I didn't like going to school. I just didn't like the whole having to sit down and having to do work and read and the whole structured thing. I wasn't disruptive or anything, I just didn't want to be there.

Lynn's remarks are evocative of John Ogbu's assertion that African Americans tend to develop an oppositional attitude toward white institutions. It also suggests a subconscious validation of Lynn's belief that minorities have a harder time achieving in school.

Even though Mary was aware of the cultural differences between American and Bolivian societies, she internalized the image of perfection that exists in the American collective psyche.

> In high school, I think I became obsessed with perfectionism because I felt I had to be better. There was something missing in my life and I didn't get it, so I had to be better. I don't know, I don't know if there was a feeling. . . . I don't know how to say this, but . . . because I didn't have what I thought I should have, I thought that maybe I contributed to not having that—that for some reason I was responsible for not having everything.

Mary's words lie at the heart of a fundamental precept of the American dominant culture, which says that individuals are ultimately responsible for their lives, regardless of circumstances, context, or other factors. Even though Mary has difficulty articulating this notion, it comes out clearly in her last statement.

Shame

Adversity can have another effect on some children: the shame of being poor or the shame of not belonging. Shame can be seen as the result of internalization.

This was particularly the case for Renée and Lori as they expressed their feelings about the social aspect of school. Renée was embarrassed to show she was on free lunch because other students made fun of her. Lori felt socially inept compared to her peers. Her small size and thick glasses made her self-conscious and intimidated by others.

Growing up Too Fast

Participants' stories suggest that adversity placed an undue burden of responsibility upon them, causing them to grow up faster than most.

Vince acquired farm and home responsibilities at the age of five or six. When her mother started working, Lori assumed her responsibilities at home.

> I have always been the kind of person who wanted to make things easier for other people, so I always tried to help make things smooth, so that when my mom came home dinner would be ready and you know, minimize the fighting and get with the other siblings about who was going to do the chores.

Renée's experience required a high level of maturity at a time when children are supposed to be taken care of. Mixed with the abuse were periods during which her mother confided in her, reversing roles between mother and daughter.

> One time she was really upset and she was just very mad and she got out a butcher knife and she said, "You know what I'm going to do, Renée? I'm just going to kill you kids, and then I'm going to kill myself and it's going to be over." I was probably twelve or thirteen then. I said, "No, no, no, put the knife away. You have to put the knife away." I finally got her to put the knife away.

When Renée finally decided to leave her mother, her father took her back to pick up her clothes. Her younger brother begged her to stay. It is unclear why her father did not take all three children away, but Renée knew she had to protect herself.

> And I was just devastated. I was thinking, I have to leave, but I can't leave him. . . . But I knew this was my only way out. I had to go. So I left and I felt horrible, horrible, horrible for doing it.

Ray had his own share of early maturity, when he attended the funeral of a mother he had never known, and later when his sister died of unknown causes.

> I remember teaching her how to read, you know, and I couldn't read a lot but I would teach her what I knew. And, the next day they told me she had passed because of something that happened in the cottage. I never went and pursued any kind of lawsuit. I just went on to say, well, I just have to pray for her now. You know, and hope that something better comes out of it. She was about thirty-six, I think. She was in her thirties.

Mark also had to grow up fast when he was left in his uncle's care upon his arrival to the United States.

Mary assumed a parental role as she took care of her little brother at home while her mother was at work. She also became her mother's parent.

> Growing up, one of the big struggles that I faced, even now, was that I became the parent, and this is very true in a lot of immigrant families where the children learn the language quicker. And my mom, although she was my mom, father, and friend, depended on me for many things. And, although I don't mind helping her, I do mind her not being independent or self-confident. So when I say things to encourage her to do it herself, she responds "Well, you don't want to help."

Self-Protection

The last category in this section refers to the respondents' tendency to create a wall around them to protect themselves from further hardship.

During her life with her mother, Renée described herself as follows:

> Actually, I never let my emotions be shown, as a general rule. People did not know I had feelings.

In an article she wrote for a publication when she was sixteen, she explained:

> I built a wall around myself to take the pain of life. I am still taking the wall down, and a new person is emerging from my shell.

Lori protected herself by drawing lessons from her experience. Talking about the relationship between her mother and her stepfather, she expressed indignation.

> And she caters to him! It's just incredible. It's a mountain women kind of thing. I don't know . . . that's a whole other story. But it actually influenced me a lot because I decided I would never marry somebody who didn't work! I am really motivated because of a lot of things.

Mark's way of protecting himself at a vulnerable time in his life was to quickly understand the dynamics of his ESL class and act upon it. Where most other students were disrespectful to the teachers, Mark showed them respect; as a result, they became fond of him.

Ray's protective shell was his theatrical side, which he still displays with enthusiasm. During the interview, he loved to imitate people. Instead of saying "Mrs. X said. . . ," he would actually portray Mrs. X, using her voice and words.

It is easy to imagine how these barriers and their effects on low-income students can represent major obstacles in a highly competitive education system such as ours. Many fall victim to such harsh forms of adversity. They become less and less motivated in school. They become either invisible or disruptive students. How, then, is it possible for children in poverty to negotiate these obstacles and change their future? The next chapter attempts to answer this question.

• 4 •

Enabling Conditions and Coping Strategies

As we saw in the preceding chapter, barriers to success profoundly affect children living in poverty, and place them at risk of academic failure, a condition that will negatively influence their chances of improving their lives in adulthood. In each of the seven stories, however, at least one condition existed that helped respondents. These conditions somehow began to reverse the effects of adversity by creating a favorable context in which they were able to beat the odds against them. In addition, respondents used specific strategies that helped them cope against adversity. In this chapter, we will examine these enabling conditions and successful strategies.

ENABLING CONDITIONS

Six conditions were identified in the stories.

- Strong family
- Support system
- Good teachers
- Caring adults
- Role models
- Turning points and significant experiences

Strong Family

A strong family helped Vince survive adversity and its effects. Vince's parents were poor but created a safe environment for their sons.

> Yes, you wore the same suit to church every Sunday morning, but you were in church every Sunday morning, including Sunday school every Sunday morning. Yes, your Dad was limited and you could tell, you know, that there were certain things that he couldn't do—you knew there were certain things he couldn't do—but you looked up to him because he was a leader in the community. He was a church leader. And there was a lot of respect and pride that came from that.

Through their quiet leadership, Vince's parents provided him (and his brothers) with a sense of security and a strong foundation.

> It was also a sense of, a feeling that because you have parents that worked together and that had a commitment and that were respected in the community, that you were always going to make it. And, that's what gave you a sense of internal security, you know, that I think probably in our family helped stabilize a lot of things.

Vince's parents valued education and encouraged him and his brothers to pursue theirs.

> Most of us in my family, with the exception of the two brothers that married very early . . . the two older brothers, were pressed by Mom and Dad. You know, some encouragement, some conversations, around trying to do better, although in telling the stories about their access to education and comparing that physically to what we had, you know, in terms of school resources, you could really see the difference. I mean, you could see and feel the difference. How they got to school and comparing that to how we got, I mean, you could see progress.

Two of Vince's brothers had a very strong positive influence on him. His third brother went on to college and came back to the community to teach social studies. His fifth brother, a very serious student who received excellent grades, also represented a role model for Vince.

Even though their lives were quite modest, the two oldest brothers, who did not graduate from high school, settled in Nebraska and offered Vince free room and board during the summer months while he was working in a commercial laundry to help pay for his and his brothers' college education.

> You know, but, it was also an opportunity for generations of the family to bond a little bit more. You know, my nieces and nephews, you know. The bonding that was able to take place there will always be with us. It will always be with us.

Mark also identified his family as a strong support system for him. Even though he did not live with them for two years, he was in the care of his father's brother, who provided the family environment Mark was missing. After two years, his parents and sisters came to the United States and encouraged him to pursue his education.

> My mother said, "No matter what you do, get an education, be a lawyer, something good." And my father as well emphasized my study. My parents never wanted me to work full-time. Actually, I never worked when I was in high school. I started working when I went to college. They both really have emphasized my studies and they have pushed me as well. So, I didn't really have any burden from my parents. They have really been supportive.

Mary also emphasizes the support her mother gave her, even though her mother could not help her. Her dream was to see both her children make it through college, and Mary has fulfilled her part of that dream.

> It was her dream to see her children do well. So much so that I remember thinking a week before my graduation from high school—I remember thinking: this graduation ceremony is not for me, it is for my mom. And realizing that what I am doing is not just for me but also for my mom and my family, my cousins, my brother. I felt that responsibility and joy as well.

Support Systems

Beyond a strong and close family, other support systems—ranging from extended family to social services, community groups, and churches—proved beneficial to the respondents.

Ray found a sense of community in the Special Olympics, a nonprofit group providing athletic activities to children and adults with mental disabilities. In the Special Olympics, Ray was treated with respect and dignity, and his performance was valued. For the first time in his life, he was given the opportunity to excel and to establish positive relationships with caring adults. Even though he dreaded going back to the institution after spending a weekend with the Special Olympics, his life became meaningful to him.

> People awarding you, hugging you, congratulating you . . . making you feel good about yourself.

During a time of homelessness, Lori, her mother, and her siblings were invited to stay with different relatives. Everyone in this extended family helped them.

> And, then, finally I guess she gave in and we went from relative to relative to relative, to stay with different relatives. So we went from brother to sister to whatever. They were all poor.

One day, Lori's uncle's house burned while they were staying with him. He was a pastor, and his church helped him rebuild his house.

> But our house burned, so both families were homeless and we went to live with relatives. My uncle had a full-time job because he was the pastor of church, so the church helped and they were reestablished right away.

Lynn chose a small circle of friends that included her cousin.

> In high school I can say that there were about two people that I probably dealt with the most and one of them was my cousin. And the other one was a girl that I met in eighth grade. She was here and my cousin and I met her together and we all decided that we would hang out and stuff, and all through high school we've been friends.

Lynn's friends were important to her. She and her friend from high school spent college freshman year together, and did not like the college so they transferred together to the same local university.

Vince found an additional source of support in his brothers who lived in Omaha, Nebraska, and who offered their homes to him during his college years, allowing him (and his other two brothers in college) to work during the summer, because there were no jobs in Mississippi.

In high school, Mark says, although everybody seemed to get along, groups tended to form based on ethnicity. He formed friendships with young men from Pakistan.

> My friends were basically from Pakistan and we were mostly guys. There weren't like a lot of Pakistani or Indian girls over there in that school.

Renée found a strong support system in undergraduate school, a small Christian college where she felt part of a caring community.

> The four years in college were the best four years of my life to that point, because my professors cared. It was a Christian college. They were

kind, caring people who really wanted to see the kids do well. And if you had any kind of desire to do well, they were just great. They were very supportive and cared that I wanted to do good and wanted to help me. It was a really supportive, great time in my life.

She also found safety and comfort in her church.

I was very, very introverted and shy. I would not force myself, you know, could not talk to people, wouldn't meet people—except in church because I felt safe there, thought people in church had to love you, they had to accept you, you know, they didn't have to at school, but they did in church.

Mary's support system was also in a church group, although she eventually left that group and discovered that the sense of community it provided was not as genuine as she had thought. She continued with that church for about five years.

Then, my second year of college, I became very frustrated with that church. The church, although it has many positive things and can work for other people, is too focused on the numbers and too structured—very rigid, and the friends that you make are friends because you're in that church, not because they are truly your friends . . . and, you don't realize that until a person is out of the church and then they banish them.

Mary also found a support system in the different high school clubs to which she belonged.

In high school, I was very popular because I was involved in different activities. At the end of the year, I was the only student that was not an athlete that was on senior trading cards. It was the first time that they had done this program. They sold trading cards to all the students and they would give these cards to elementary schools.

The Early Identification Program was another source of support that eventually gave Mary the opportunity to attend college with a full four-year scholarship.

I used to attend the summer academies since the time I was in the eighth grade to the time I graduated. And, each year, students—about sixty—are chosen for that reason, I believe, to make sure that they can beat the odds.

Good Teachers

While school may represent a hostile environment, from grade school through college, respondents met good teachers along the way. These teachers had two common characteristics: they made their students feel better about themselves and they motivated them academically.

Vince remembered his first teacher, Ethel Simpson, with fondness and respect. He also recognized his tenth-grade teacher who pushed him to excel as much as his fifth brother. Finally, his own brother (the third one) became his social studies and government teacher for one year and motivated Vince to push himself academically.

Lori was blessed with many such teachers in elementary school; in high school, Miss Darla seemed to stand out.

> In high school, Miss Darla—this picture you see on the wall . . . the white-haired lady—that picture is when she was ninety-three. She came to a dinner honoring me in the fall. She flew up from Georgia, at ninety-four. She taught me algebra, geometry, trigonometry, Latin, and she was the honor society's advisor. She really became a mentor to me though she may not have realized it. And she encouraged me; helped me to apply for college.

Ray was fond of his music teacher at City Home because he liked music and felt safe with her. He was fortunate to establish a special connection with her by working outside the classroom, performing for other residents at City Home.

> She was just an amazing person. And many people wanted to stay and hang out with her. And I got a chance to work with her like I was telling you about, the cottages that didn't have a lot of recreation and activities. I got a chance to work with her at City Home. It was me and a couple other students assisting her in music and entertaining and showing all the keys about music and sounds, and waving your hands, and the Hokey Pokey, and stuff like that. I felt good.

Renée, Mark, and Mary did not identify any specific teachers with whom they established a privileged relationship.

Mrs. Smith was one of Lynn's good teachers, but she was "mean." Lynn was grateful to her, though, for keeping her focused. Lynn also remembers a good math teacher who helped her pass her state Literacy Passport test, but she seems to have made a lesser impression on Lynn.

Other Caring Adults

Beside good teachers, other adults were able to provide respondents with a safe, if temporary, haven from adversity.

Vince found a surprising source of support in the white owners of the laundry where he and his two college brothers worked during the summer in Nebraska.

> The people that owned the laundry that we used to work in were people that grew up in Mississippi. When the connection was made to Mississippi it was just something that they expected us to do every summer month. And, if we didn't call them, they would call us. And, you know, the way we were able to connect with them and talk about things—you know, talk about what we were doing in college and the support that was there from those people were quite touching. You had to literally work for everything that you got but they gave you the opportunity to work. They were very encouraging about it all. And although you had to work very hard, you know, it was very uncomfortable, but it was also uplifting because of the interest and the connection that they made to what we were doing and trying to do, you know, as family.

At a time when race relations were still governed by a rigid system of inequality, the owners of the laundry started reversing what Vince had come to expect from Caucasians, showing that whites could indeed be caring people.

Lori's grandfather was her greatest admirer, who loved her regardless of what she was doing or not doing.

> One of the things I think that was very positive through the whole thing that though my grandfather, my mother's dad, was not an educated man at all—in fact he probably had little to no formal education, I'm not sure if he even went to grade school, maybe a year—was one of the most nurturing and loving people and he really felt that if God made the earth and only put one person on it, it would have probably been me. You know? I mean he just . . . so having somebody who thought you were just God's gift to the world was—and he always did until the day he died—I mean, he thought I was . . . it was totally unassociated with my success academically or anything . . . it was just who I was as a person.

Lori had a friend in high school whose parents were very kind and caring, picking Lori up for school functions, including her in their daughter's activities, and taking her to ball games.

For Ray, these caring adults were Eunice Shriver, founder of the Special Olympics, and her team of volunteers, who managed to give Ray much-needed affection while encouraging him to become self-reliant. Ray described how Mrs. Shriver and her staff would talk to him after a loss.

> So, I had to learn through Special Olympics that that's not how the Special Olympics are, and Ms. Shriver was . . . she was a tough lady. "Come here. What's the matter?" You know, that's how she was . . . she was just like that type of lady. You'd wipe the tears and you try to tell her what happened and she'd give you some encouragement, but the hugs I thought were real good.

Mark's uncle emerged as the most prominent caring adult in his youth, after he was left in the care of his uncle when he was eleven.

Renée's father was the most important caring adult in her childhood. Even though he left his family, he cared deeply for her and eventually saved her from her mother's abuse. His presence is felt as very caring throughout Renée's story. He rescued her, obtained custody of her, encouraged her to stay in school and apply herself to her studies, and helped her as much as he could financially. He was protective of her, and even when he did not agree with her choices, he would not oppose them. Without her father, it is difficult to imagine how Renée would have been able to achieve all that she has.

Lynn and Mary both had very close relationships with their mothers. Lynn's mother supported the family by being a foster parent. When Lynn was having difficulty in school, she would first call her mother to let her know she had received a bad grade on a test.

Mary's mother was also very close to her. Mary credited her mother for believing in her ability to succeed. She appears as an extremely caring yet vulnerable adult, with whom Mary sometimes reversed roles.

> I have always received that positive reinforcement from my mom: you're intelligent, you're strong, you're going to change the fate of our family. You are special, you are wonderful, you are my jewel. She always gave a positive feeling and I know that this is true. I had to believe whatever I was told.

Role Models

Caring adults and role models did not appear to be necessarily the same people in the respondents' lives. For instance, Mary's mother was the most caring adult in her life, yet she herself did not have an education beyond tenth grade. Lori's grandfather was not a role model but simply someone who cared for her unconditionally.

Role models were individuals who actually inspired respondents to follow in their steps. Vince's parents modeled "quiet leadership" in the face of adversity. His third brother was the first son to go to college and became a teacher, and he was instrumental in helping their parents acquire their own farm.

Lori's math teacher and honor society advisor, Miss Darla, whose picture hangs in Lori's office, inspired her to go to college, graduate, and teach for a few years.

> She really became a mentor to me though she may not have realized it. And encouraged me, helped me to apply for college.

Turning Points

In all the respondents' lives, there came a time when they experienced (to varying degrees) a significant moment that changed the direction of their lives.

Vince's turning point took place when he was challenged by his teacher in tenth grade to become motivated about his education. Until then, by his own admission, Vince had been doing well but with no effort.

Lori's significant moment came when Miss Darla, her math teacher, asked her if she would apply to go to college.

Renée's breakthrough was the day when, braving her fear of being rejected, she found the courage to call her dad for help, and he came and rescued her. Once in his care, she was able to focus on her academic work and think about her future.

Mark's turning point happened when he found a way to reach out to his teachers despite his limited English proficiency.

Lynn's significant experience took place when her best friend had a baby and dropped out of school, provoking in Lynn a determination to make a different choice for herself.

Ray's unique opportunity was to become involved with the Special Olympics. In addition, the closing of City Home ended a very painful chapter in his life.

Mary's turning point happened when she entered the Early Identification Program, which eventually led her to a four-year full scholarship.

COPING STRATEGIES

In the preceding section, we identified the conditions that provided respondents with opportunities to address or reverse the effects of adversity. This section examines the different strategies respondents adopted to make use of these opportunities and overcome adversity.

They are:

- Perseverance
- Resistance
- Friendly competitiveness
- Faith and spirituality
- Putting a positive spin on the journey
- Creating distance

Perseverance

This category refers to the continued efforts respondents made when faced with adversity. Respondents simply did not give up. They persisted in different areas.

Vince showed perseverance when he reached graduate school and faced stiff competition from privileged students. His model of perseverance existed in his parents.

> My parents were not vocal people, but they had a lot of quiet strength and determination that things could be better for us.

Vince did not give up, and persevered at the University of Illinois until he received his master's degree.

> The competition was tremendous there. It was obvious that certain people had been exposed to certain research skills and techniques and tools that I had not been exposed to. I had to learn both the tools and the trade plus do the research and that alone set you back somewhat.

After discovering on her first day at school that she did not know elementary things that she was supposed to know, Lori learned them that first evening.

> So, of course, the second day of school, I knew how to do all those things because I was a determined child.

In high school, when Lori had social difficulties, she took a lot of extra classes.

> My friends were all dating and all kinds of stuff. It was just really hard for me. I just kind of poured myself into my schoolwork.

When, during a discussion with her mother about race, she discovered a enormous difference of views between her and her family, she "charged forth and they stayed the same." She decided to apply for and go to college, despite her mother's lack of support.

> It was very emotional because I remember going home to say to her that I had spent time talking to Miss Darla about going to college and Mom said, "I don't know what college is." So, I sat down, did the whole thing, explained, and I said, "Miss Darla thinks I should go to college and I'd like to be a teacher, I think, and come back and help people in school because I had some people who helped me." And my mom just sat and cried and she said, "Well I don't know what it means and it's a big change and nobody's ever done this before." And she said, "You know, I can't help you." She wouldn't even help me fill out the forms. And she said, "I don't know how to help you fill out the forms and I don't know how to advise you if you should go or not. I don't want you to go away."

Today, Lori still shows her perseverance by serving "the people everyone else has given up on."

Mark persevered for two years in a new country without his parents.

Renée endured abuse until she was fifteen years old. Then, with no study habits to speak of, she applied herself to college and eventually earned a master's degree in counseling. Despite the abuse, she never severed the relationship with her mother.

Ray's endurance showed in the years he survived at City Home. In addition, when he found the Special Olympics and the opportunity to apply himself to athletic activities in a safe environment, he showed such perseverance that he won medals for his performance.

Today at age forty-one, he attends the Kennedy Institute Night School and hopes to earn a high school diploma. "I am trying to get back a lot of the education I lost when I was [at City Home]." Ray believes that a person with a disability has more perseverance than others.

> It's harder for them to get a job because of their disability. But an average person will go out there, fill the application, start tomorrow and leave two days after tomorrow, where a person with a disability may stay forever.

Lynn persevered through an institution (school) in which she did not feel comfortable. Her willpower helped her eventually go to college, and her choice of career shows her desire to address social injustice and her conviction that it can happen, despite a hostile environment for African Americans.

Mary knew she was a good student. She was placed at the top of her first-grade class in Bolivia, but when she came to the United States she was placed in lower tracks because of language barriers. She persevered and eventually won a four-year full scholarship in college.

Resistance

While all seven respondents showed perseverance, only Ray and Lynn's stories showed some evidence of resistance, a more oppositional form of persistence.

Ray felt at times that he had to resist his environment, even though it meant he would be punished for fighting.

Lynn's resistance to what she saw as a racial divide showed in her choice of a career in administration of justice. Her resistance was also evidenced in her thoughts about institutions in general, and schools in particular. Her opposition to school ("I hated school") and to the justice system ("probation officers are mean") was evident in her responses.

To a lesser extent, Lori also exercised resistance against her mother's resentment that she was applying for college. She did not let her mother's reaction discourage her.

Friendly Competitiveness

Ray, Mark, Mary, and Vince used competitiveness as a strategy to reach their goals. They engaged in athletic or intellectual activities that gave them an edge over others.

Ray discovered the Special Olympics, which provided a safe environment in which he could excel in track and field. The Special Olympics web site indicates that the organization believes that "competition among those of equal abilities is the best way to test its athletes' skills, measure their progress and inspire them to grow."

> That's how I started. Exercising, training, shouting out, encouraging, making all that noise, and hoping that I'd win; I hate to lose. Had to learn the fundamentals about winning and losing.

Ray learned that it was okay to lose and that what mattered most was to give his best efforts.

When Mary first attended school in the U.S. and was assigned lower-track classes, she developed a strong sense of competition not so much against others as against herself.

> And, in that academy [Early Identification], I became very competitive. Everything I did was to compete against my peers. But also besides that competitiveness, I was pushing myself. I tried to read more books than I was assigned. I tried to learn other things, not in the classroom, because I felt—I felt I wasn't given all of that. So that's why I wanted to learn more. I think I became obsessed with that.

Mark's sense of competitiveness motivated him to graduate from high school one year early. After a friend of his graduated in eleventh grade, he decided he could do it too.

Until tenth grade, Vince had been a good student, but did not make any special effort in school. His teacher appealed to his sense of competition against his brother to motivate Vince.

> I sort of had the attitude I could do things but I didn't want to. And there was a strong male teacher and he would always do a comparison where I was to where my brother was and I think I sort of got tired of it one day. I thought, "Hmm, I think I'll show you!" I think that person knew a little bit about me and my potential. How he went about doing the comparative stuff was motivating, you know. And, that sort of gave me the lift that I needed to apply myself a little bit more. And once you start making those As and start receiving recognition, you say, "Wow, I think I'll sort of continue to do this" because you really get hooked by it. I sort of got hooked by it, and I thank him a lot for it. And, you also get hooked by, you know, when you see your parents' eyes light up and the fact that other people—particularly at that time—respect you for it. And I think that that gave me the boost that I needed to apply myself a little bit more.

Faith and Spirituality

Faith and spirituality often helped respondents to transcend their difficulty and suffering by acknowledging their own lack of power to change the present, and by allowing them to dream of a brighter future.

Vince acknowledged the role of black churches in the '60s to inspire and empower African American communities.

> But, you know, the strength of the black families and more importantly the strength of which they got from their church is what I think carried the day. It really is what I think carried the day at that time. The church was the place where people came together. And they believed in what they were doing. And, you know, they believed if they stayed together and they kept to the principle of nonviolence, you know, that things would happen over time. And I saw that in the leadership around my little area.

Vince does not talk about his own faith but his parents' faith, and his father's role in the local church gave him the strength to carry on.

From the very beginning, Lori felt a strong sense of faith, which she associates with feeling different and questioning things.

> My faith has always been a very strong part of my life and when I felt like everything else failed, it was a very substantial source of strength to me. . . . I always was asking questions and kind of challenging what's going on in this world and why are things different. And so I think that there was obviously a work for me to do and for whatever reason, I feel like my whole life was a preparation for what I'm doing now.

When asked what helped him overcome adversity in his life, Ray answers:

> I think, I guess, my spiritual side; each time I pray, I know something good is going to happen. The spiritual side I think has helped us [Ray and his wife] a lot. And knowing that God can provide, do all things, and through the courage of many other ones who have a disability that you can overcome and you can achieve some goals. Because a lot of times they think that a disability is a disability, you won't go nowhere but here. That's not true. You can do a lot more, if you put your heart into it.

Like Lori, Ray did not rely solely on his faith to provide him with everything, but used it as a foundation for self-help and for helping others within the community of people with disabilities.

Renée's faith not only saved her from the psychological scars of her mother's abuse but also helped stop the cycle of violence and hatred that usually runs from one generation to another.

Mary was born in the Catholic faith but became involved in a nondenominational church in the United States—a church that helped her to become goal-oriented and provided her with a context of structured activities, friends, and mentors that were needed at that time. A few years later she left that church, but her faith in God remained intact. Asked what helped her beat the odds against her, she answers:

> I had a distinct belief, a spiritual belief, that God wanted something better for me. I think that was what motivated me. I left that church because of my personal belief but it's not just that church that believes in God; there are different ways of worshipping God or honoring God and learning about him.

Neither Mark nor Lynn referred to their faith or spiritual side or God as something that helped them in their journey to success. This does not necessarily mean it was not there; they may have considered this side of them too private to share with me.

Putting an Optimistic Spin on the Journey

Three of the respondents felt that, despite poverty and other forms of adversity, they were better off than others or simply that things were not that bad after all. This, they said, helped them overcome their own difficulties.

After describing his family life on the farm where his parents were sharecroppers, racial segregation in his community, and the lack of resources, Vince added:

> But let me also put another spin to this. Although all of those things happened in terms of the economic struggle, you know, it was hard for us to think at that time that we were really living in poverty.

Mark thought that while Asian schools were superior to American schools academically, American schools were better than Asian schools. He felt that he ended up in the better system by immigrating to the U.S.

> I would say that the level of Asian schools or the level of Asian education is higher than in the U.S., but the system here in the U.S. is better than the Asian system. One good thing about the United States is that whoever wants to study at whatever age can do it, which is good.

Ray sometimes felt privileged and better off than others at City Home.

> I thought we had it bad, but then when I saw there were some cottages where there were supposed to be children with severe mental retardation and they needed doctors on hand for that. They didn't have it like we had it. They were more isolated. They didn't get a chance to go to the movies, go shopping, do the things that we were doing.

Creating Distance

This category refers to a set of actions by which the respondents created for themselves a physical, geographical, emotional, and/or intellectual space away from the conditions that represented adversity. They all eventually left to establish a life of their own. Lynn announced that she would do the same as soon as possible. By doing so, they removed themselves from the contexts that carried the causes of their difficulties.

Before they physically left, some respondents indicated that they had already left in their minds. Mark, for whom the first years of school in the U.S. represented a context of adversity, chose not to associate with groups he perceived as negative. Instead, he chose to stay with a group from Pakistan.

Ray and his friends were all trying to apply for a transfer to another cottage where residents were more independent.

> We had a cottage that was supposed to be more like an independent building where you were able to go out on Saturdays. They had it made up there. On Saturdays, they got to go out on their own and shop and buy things and be more independent. And that's what we were working towards.

Later, he seized an opportunity to attend special education classes in a school outside the institution.

> They were able to take some of us that were in institutions out of the institutions to mainstream them into regular schools so we could get used to a job, learn how to get a job, stuff like that.

Lori knew she had to leave the area physically and psychologically.

> I haven't spent a lot of time feeling sorry for myself. I think there are a lot of people who never get over whatever it is. And I just said, you

> know, get on with life; now that you are an adult, you can behave in different ways, you can think different thoughts. I think the other thing that has helped me to be really successful is moving out of the area.

Surprisingly, Lori did not to attend her own graduations from college or graduate school, citing practical reasons. As the first person in her family to graduate, one might have expected her to mark these unique occasions for self-satisfaction. While these do not necessarily indicate a sense of distance on her part, they confirm her sense of modesty about her accomplishments. By not attending her own graduation ceremonies, she perhaps avoided having to become emotional about her painful journey to achievement.

Mary struggled between an emotional attachment to her cultural roots with Bolivia and her desire to succeed in this country. While she was and still is very attached to her mother, she also created a space for herself that was very different from home. The church to which she converted gave her discipline, goals, a structure, and group activities that her home did not provide.

• 5 •

The Experience of Achievement

After years of navigating personal and institutional obstacles, our respondents reached a new milestone: the experience of achievement. This chapter describes the respondents' experience of achievement and the effects achievement had on them, as well as on others around them. They also share in retrospect their insights into the process of resilience.

AWARDS AND RECOGNITIONS

After being pushed by one of his teachers, Vince applied himself to his studies. He graduated from high school, went to a local college, spent a few semesters at the University of Tulane, and then was accepted to graduate school at the University of Illinois. Exposure to more challenges was key to Vince's success.

From the beginning, Lori was a high achiever in school. Pushed by one of her teachers to apply for college, she was accepted with a scholarship and graduated in just over three years, then earned her graduate degree in mathematics from Duke University.

A perfect example of what educators call "an invisible child," Renée never thought she would go to college. After taking college preparatory classes, she was accepted at a small Christian college and decided to pursue a graduate degree in counseling. While in college, she earned the "service above self" award, which recognized students who had volunteered their time.

> I had never once considered that I would ever be a recipient of any award. They called my name and I was just sitting there. People were saying, "Renée, that's you, go, go, go, go!" And finally I got up but I was in shock.

Mark graduated from high school at the end of his junior year, and went on to college to study managing information systems.

Coming from a single-parent family, caught in a cycle of poverty, and living in a society where minority status is stigmatized, Lynn graduated from high school and went on to college to study administration of justice.

Mary learned English and adjusted to the United States. Despite poverty, initial illegal residency status, a single-parent family, sharing one room with her mother and brother, she prevailed and is currently pursuing a double major in college on a full scholarship. She intends to go to graduate school.

Ray is the only participant in the study who did not achieve in formal schooling, although he is still working toward that goal. His achievement is in the area of service, leadership, and building awareness about people with disabilities. He was recognized by Washington, D.C., Mayor Marion Barry for overcoming obstacles in his life.

PARENTS' REACTIONS TO ACHIEVEMENT

Vince, Mark, Mary, and Lynn's families reacted very positively to their success, whereas Lori's parents were indifferent to it. Renée's father supported her, but her mother did not think school had any significant role to play in Renée's life. Ray's parents were not a part of his life.

EFFECTS OF ACHIEVEMENT ON THE RESPONDENTS

Without a doubt, success became an important part of the respondents' lives at some stage. While most of them were exhilarated by it, some felt anxiety mixed with happiness.

Lori's acceptance to college made her anxious because it caused tension between her and her family. Vince's academic success made him proud and challenged him to continue, but when he reached graduate school and realized what his competition was, anxiety settled in. Lynn was always a good student, yet she hated school. Her success must have generated a conflict for her. Mary did not feel that she had achieved success yet.

Ray is not quite satisfied about his academic level and is still studying to earn his GED. He experiences schools through his son, who is currently in seventh grade. He thinks highly of schools but also points to a troubling aspect of them at the middle level. They are too impersonal and too inattentive to individual students.

> You kind of get lost in a lot of the schools when you get up to a certain level like the seventh grade. You are kind of lost. You have more responsibilities and you don't get any warning about that. It's really a waste of time. Children lose out.

Without exception, achievement despite adversity made all respondents very sensitive to the struggles of others. Lori, Vince, Lynn, and Renée chose careers that focused on service to others. Mary did not say what kind of career she was interested in.

LOOKING BACK

Respondents looked back on their journey in three different ways: by often remembering, by helping others, and—not unlike Victor Frankl—by searching and finding meaning to their experiences.

Remembering

Looking back to his years in City Home, Ray remembers those who died before the institution was forced to close its doors. He sometimes goes back to the cemetery adjacent to the property and recalls his sister and friends.

Lori goes back to where she grew up, but not too often. When she remembers her past, she feels that it prepared her for what she is doing now—taking care of people in need.

Vince remembers the struggles, the inequities, the Civil Rights movement, its leaders, the hope and fear it inspired, and his family, still the most important people in his life.

Mark and Mary remember the struggle to adjust; Lynn remembers her friend who dropped out of high school because she was pregnant.

Renée is now expecting her first baby and remembers the fear of the abuse, and the strength that education gave her.

Helping Others

Ray wants to help children with disabilities.

> What I want to do when I leave Special Olympics, I told them, what I want to do is to be able to go back and to work with some of the little children, especially, to give them some encouragement. So when they get older they will feel good about themselves. And we hear more and more success stories.

Lori made her whole life a life of service to those who are at the bottom of the social ladder.

> Because of where I've been, I feel there's hope for every person. I love to serve the people everybody has given up on. They don't fit in a shelter, they can't do the county programs, they've been kicked out of housing, they've done whatever, and they're failures by society's standards. It gives me tremendous gratification to be present to that person and really begin to understand what that person could be if somebody only formed a relationship and encouraged them to grow. That's my life. I really feel I can see hope for every person, no matter how bad it is.

Mark dreams of helping his family once he launches his career, by buying a home for his family, and by relieving his father's obligation to work full-time.

Renée provides counseling services to people in need.

Finding Meaning

In remembering their recent or not-so-recent past, all participants found meaning in their journey from poor working-class to middle-class socioeconomic status. In their effort to explain and analyze inequities, discrimination, poverty, abuse, and hostility, they also found reconciliation with their past and lessons for the future.

Vince feels fortunate to have grown up at the time of the Civil Rights movement, when black families were still intact for the most part, and drugs had not invaded urban communities. Ironically, today things look bleaker to Vince.

> I have obviously been more fortunate than some others have been, but I won't consider myself as being totally realizing the American Dream until I can be in the position to give a lot more back to my community.

> And it's just not in "my community" in terms of my hometown, but it's my community period. I want to be able to make sure, you know, that they have the exposure and the opportunities and the start that I didn't have. You know, that will allow them to go a lot further and take it a lot further in terms of being corporate leaders of the future, being community leaders of the future, than perhaps I have. And if we're able to do a lot more of that, then I think we will come closer over the next generation to realizing some of those dreams. But I just want to emphasize again, things like drugs and the breakdown of the family, and the rate of incarceration of my people is frightening. It is absolutely frightening. From cities to small towns, and that to me is what our leadership has got to focus on. The leadership of traditional community and civil rights organizations has got to focus on this issue a lot more than they have in the past. Otherwise, that dream is going to get further and further and further away.

Through her own story, Lori discovered that the most important thing that can happen to anyone in society is bonding with someone else. This is essentially what she provides at Community Service. She was meeting with the staff of a homeless shelter one day, and the staff was describing the difficulty they had in dealing with their residents because Lori's organization had established too strong a bond with the homeless people in the shelter.

> I think the most important thing I'd say is that they [people living in poverty] have to be able to form some sort of relationship with other people. And I'm real keen on that because of the homeless that we see. And I just had this discussion at the shelter the other day when we went over to talk to the shelter people and they were actually complaining that our social workers are so close to the clients when they're in the home, working on the streets here with them, and then when they go into the shelters they don't want to work with the shelter people. And I said, I think that's actually a very positive thing. I mean, do you understand that they bonded with us, therefore they can bond with you? It means you're going to have to do a little bit of work, but a whole lot less work than we had to do because they had no bonding relationship. And I think that any growth that happens, whether you're three or sixty, really depends on relationships. I think relationships are everything.

Ray still has a lot of unanswered questions about life at City Home, but he knows what he wants: to educate society about people with disabilities, and to help children with disabilities so they don't have to suffer as much as he did.

> When I look at those years, I remember the school that I attended and how I wish there had been a lot more that we could have done instead of sitting in a classroom just being bored. Then I look back at a lot of my friends who didn't get a chance to come out who passed on and are at the cemetery. On Memorial Day no one cares a hoot; their families don't come to visit, no flowers, no nothing. It's like they are just there—that's history. Sometimes I go back and I think that you can never forget those, you know, because if they were living they would have been out too. And I look back at my older sister; I look back at her thinking what would she do if she had gotten out. Would she have been free or still in?
>
> I look back at all those things. I can never forget that I lived there. I have to tell them, I know sometimes people say, "Oh, he's not going to say that again." I say, "I have to say it. I'm a former resident of an institution, and that's me." Sometimes there are people, like on the Mayor's Committee, who say, "Please don't say that. Just say that you're here to represent the Special Olympics."

Renée found meaning to her childhood through education and her faith. With both in her life, she knows the abuse in her family will stop with her. When she was alone in graduate school, she started counting her blessings.

> I remember one Thanksgiving I was there. I was going to be alone because I didn't have enough money to go home, and the lady I was living with was going to visit her children. That was my first holiday completely alone. My friends were going home for the holidays and I didn't want to impose on anyone. So, I went into a little moping thing there, you know, and then I thought, "Renée, think of all the things you have to be thankful for." It's then that I started counting my blessings instead and changed my mood. It was neat because that experience showed me that I was not going to get into a situation where God was going let me fall down after where I'd come from, you know. He was not going to say, "Oh, I got you here! {Click} Down the stairs you go!"

Mark not only reconciled himself with his initial culture shock, but also advises others to do the same.

> This advice is not just for the children, it is for the adults as well who come here from different nations, from different countries. We all go through the same process when new families come here from different countries. They see people who have cars, they see people who have houses, they see people who are living in apartments, and who are doing okay. And then they see you, "Oh, these people have everything and we

> don't." And, how are they going to work? At the beginning this is hard. It's not an easy life over here, especially for those who don't have a good education. But I can guarantee that everyone can settle down here after a while. In the beginning, it's hard because people don't know what's going on, they don't know what's happening. It takes a year and a half or two to settle down. In the beginning it may seem impossible, but it will take strength and courage, then it gets better. And I'm sure that whoever comes here could and would live a good life after a while. After struggling, the results are here.

Lynn took a hard-line approach to her life. Given the cards she was dealt, she still had a choice to make: do well in school or drop out, have a baby, become delinquent. She made her choice and so should others.

Cross-cultural understanding is a major theme in Mary's analysis of her childhood.

> Because I grew up in the United States, I adapted a lot of what is considered American culture although American culture in itself is extremely diverse. So there is a very strong sense of being future-oriented and I have become "Americanized." I've become acculturated to this culture from a very early age—six years old—and I had no other choice but to learn. On the other hand, I don't consider myself an American. I think about it and I say, "Maybe in the future I will become an American." Maybe the dynamics of the United States will change so that the Americanization process will include also bicultural ways of thinking. I think that Latinos are also American even if they weren't born here, if they have the American culture. If they live here as citizens, they are American. I also believe that because, besides Native Americans, everyone else has that same history. On the other hand, there are a lot of things that I don't share with American values. And, of course, that's from growing up in a different country. If it were up to me, I would be more family-oriented. I would be definitely more present-oriented . . . more focused on the people and the relationships with the people. I can relate to and I share more with international people than I do with people that were born here. I share more with the people that have struggled in their personal lives than I do with the mainstream white American.

SUMMARY AND CONCLUSION

The cross-case analysis of the seven participants' stories reveals a complex network of factors associated with resilience.

First, the study shows that adversity takes on many faces. While poverty certainly represents one of them, it is often the compounding of poverty with other factors, or the factors associated with lack of financial resources, that create an environment not conducive to academic achievement. As the study reveals, these factors can be the stigmatization of racial and ethnic identity; a sense of physical or mental isolation; lack of exposure to educational opportunities; various hostile environments including family, social, economic, and political contexts; the difficulty associated with learning how to learn; the lack of congruence between school and life; and other personal or institutional barriers to success.

Second, adversity affects self-concept. Respondents were affected in different and complex ways. They became fearful, anxious, resentful, and sometimes ashamed of their condition. These feelings could turn inward as they internalized the label(s) projected upon them. Adversity also caused them to grow out of childhood too fast in order to assume adult responsibilities. They also became distant and guarded in an attempt to protect themselves against an environment that was hostile to them.

Third, respondents identified certain conditions that contributed to alleviate the worst effects of adversity. Strong families and other support systems (extended families, friends, church groups, grassroots organizations), good teachers, other caring adults, and role models provided a circle of safety in which participants could then begin to effect change in their lives. Turning points and breakthroughs also made it possible for them to imagine better lives.

Fourth, respondents adopted certain strategies that helped them beat the odds against them. All showed perseverance through hardship. Other strategies included fighting back (resistance), engaging in friendly competition, living their faith, putting a positive spin on their journey, and accepting the challenge. Most also removed themselves physically or mentally from the context that carried adversity.

The cross-case analysis also reveals that achievement can take different faces, and that with success comes new challenges, such as a sense of separation or alienation from families or friends, or a sense of belonging to two different worlds.

Finally, the study reveals how participants found meaning in their life experiences.

• 6 •

Conclusion

How did the seven participants find their way from adversity to success and beyond? Table 6–1 illustrates the different phases of this journey.

They are represented under the titles: (1) Barriers to success (the different forms of adversity respondents had to face in their lives); (2) Effects of adversity (the different ways adversity affected the respondents); (3) Enabling conditions (the environments and factors that empowered respondents); (4) Coping strategies (the different characteristics and strategies respondents adopted to fight against adversity); (5) Achievement (the different forms and experiences of success); and (6) Looking back (the reflections and analyses offered by the respondents as they looked back on their struggles and ultimate victories).

Within each category, subcategories emerged and are represented in table 6-1 in individual boxes under each category title.

What lessons can we draw from the lives of our participants in this study? Certainly their stories are inspiring and humbling at the same time. The wisdom they gained through their experiences of adversity and resilience is remarkable. There is, however, another level of understanding of their stories, a level that reaches deep into our social and cultural values and habits, a level where we as a society can learn some valuable lessons and draw some conclusions for the future. This final chapter attempts to unveil and discuss this deeper level of analysis. It will cover two topics: first, it will provide a link back to the research on resilience; and second, it will discuss the implications of this study for those interested in bridging the educational achievement gap between privileged and underprivileged students in American schools.

Table 6-1 Resilience Among Low-Income Achievers

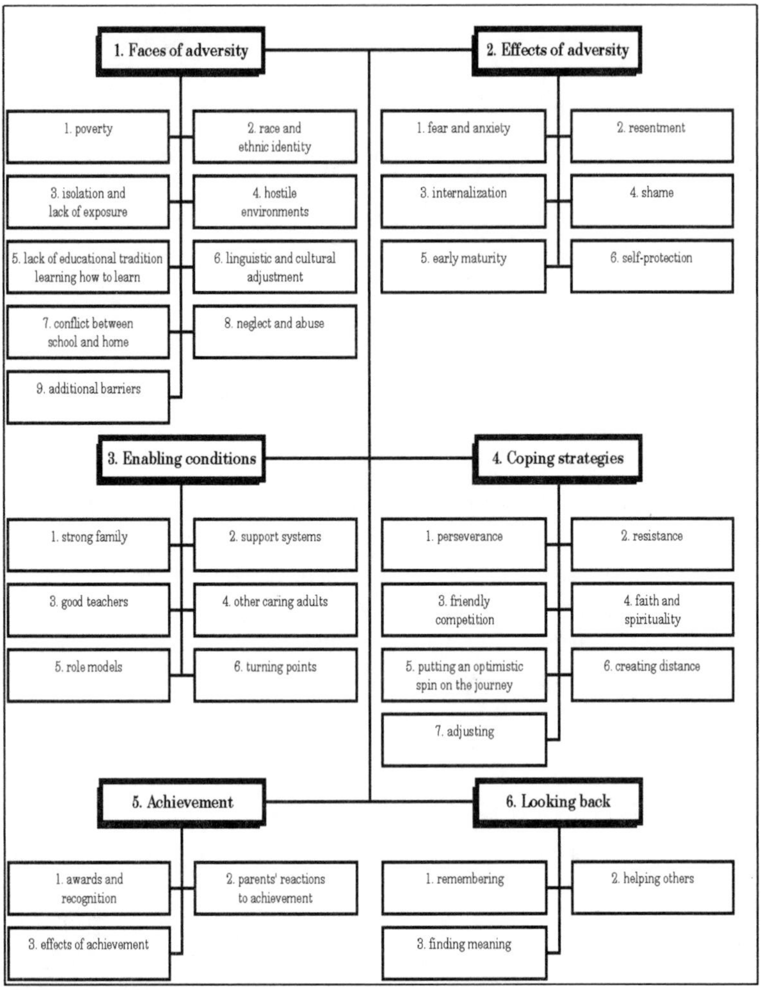

LINK TO EXISTING RESEARCH ON RESILIENCE

We saw in chapter 3 that adversity for poor, working-class people can take many forms. All respondents were aware of at least one salient form of adversity in their lives: for Ray, being confined to an institution; for Vince, poverty and racial segregation; for Lori, poverty and isolation; for Renée, poverty and an abusive mother; for Mark and Mary, poverty and cultural and linguistic adaptation; and for Lynn, stigmatization of poverty and being an African American. With the exception of Ray, all respondents agreed that poverty had played a major role in their childhood and school experience by compounding other forms of adversity and by stigmatizing them.

As the study progressed and participants revealed their life stories, their experiences started resonating in my mind and echoing some of the authors who had contributed to the literature and research on resilience. It occurred to me that each could indeed be associated with one of these authors either by way of illustration or by opposition. The authors that came to my mind were Mike Rose, Richard Rodriguez, Victor Frankl, Mary Gibson, Ray McDermott and Hervé Varenne, John Ogbu, and Jonathan Kozol. These authors represent a comprehensive range of thoughts on issues of adversity and resilience among poor, working-class Americans.

Mike Rose

In *Lives on the Boundary,* Mike Rose draws upon his personal experience as a young student and the stories of his students at UCLA to discuss "America's educational underclass." Rose gives an account of his childhood and schooling in one of the poorest areas of Los Angeles in the '50s. His strength of analysis, enriched by his own story and his interactions with students who are crossing the boundary of social class, represented a natural complement to this study. Salient issues in *Lives on the Boundary* include poverty (financial and educational), inspiring teachers or mentors, labeling and its effects on students, and turning points.

All seven respondents in this study could relate to Mike Rose. Their lives echo Rose's account of his own experience as a student and his encounters with underprepared students.

Richard Rodriguez

Richard Rodriguez came to mind when I heard the testimonies of Mary and Lori. Mary both confirmed and disconfirmed Rodriguez's assertions in *Hunger of Memory*. She almost sounded like an echo to Rodriguez when she referred to her obsession with goals, especially when she mentioned that one of her goals in high school was to read all of Shakespeare. She was, however, very different from him when it came to the issues of her family or culture and language. Unlike Rodriguez, she was and still is very attached to her family—especially her mother—and while she felt the tension between what Rodriguez calls the public (Anglo) versus intimate

(Hispanic) cultures, she has no intention of letting go of the latter, as Rodriguez did.

Lori, on the other hand, did remind me of Rodriguez because, like him, she felt a chasm form between herself and her family and decided to move on, leaving her family "behind," almost as the price to pay for her own social deliverance. While Lori is Anglo-American, her educational journey took her out of her culture of origin (rural Georgia) in a manner evocative of Rodriguez's own educational journey.

Ray McDermott and Hervé Varenne

McDermott and Varenne focused part of their research on the effects of labeling on students. Ray and Mary both reminded me of these two authors. Mary came to mind because she became aware of the label that was cast upon her as a foreign student when she entered elementary school. Ray in particular reminded me of Adam in "Adam, Adam, Adam, and Adam," a student labeled learning disabled who became the object of intense observation by the two authors. In four different social situations, Adam became four different individuals. Adam spent a great deal of energy trying to fight off the label he had been assigned and was rather successful in everyday social situations, when he could apply his skills without the fear of the label. However, he was less successful at fighting off his label in more structured contexts, like classes or when taking a test. McDermott and Varenne concluded that school contributed immensely to Adam's problem, by creating a label (learning disabled) that became the lens through which others (his peers, his teachers, and even his parents) saw him.

In a striking parallel to Adam's story, Ray was diagnosed mentally retarded and condemned to carrying this label for years until he was able to find a new social context (Special Olympics) in which he was allowed to become a different Ray.

Margaret Gibson

In *Accommodation without Assimilation*, Margaret Gibson describes how a Sikh community of new immigrants faces the obstacle of cultural adaptation in a hostile environment. Persistence and non-assimilation represent the two most powerful strategies used by this ethnic group to push through the system with remarkable results. Mark's story represents a fitting illustration of Gibson's findings.

Victor Frankl

Ray and Renée, through their stories of sheer survival, embodied the type of resilience and search for understanding experienced by Frankl. In both stories (as in Frankl's account of survival), life itself became uncertain at times and the context in which they lived could be seen as a type of concentration camp.

John Ogbu

Anthropologist John Ogbu devised a theory to explain differences in achievement among minority groups. He called it Cultural Model. According to this theory, the difference between minorities who (collectively) succeed in school and those who don't is that:

> The former possess a cultural model or understanding of the working of American society and their place in it that is more conducive to school success. And the difference in the cultural models arises from differences in the histories of the minorities.

Two factors influence the differences in cultural models mentioned by Ogbu: first, the "initial terms of incorporation into the United States;" and second, what Ogbu calls "patterns of responses [these groups] make to subsequent treatment by white Americans." Involuntary immigrants cannot compare their present situation to a "back home" situation as voluntary immigrants do. They also perceive their situation of oppression as permanent and develop an oppositional social identity vis-à-vis the white majority, whereas voluntary immigrants perceive the same situation as temporary and develop a different social identity vis-à-vis the white majority.

Mark and Mary can be viewed as "voluntary immigrants" in Ogbu's theory. Indeed, they both had an initial adaptation period in which they struggled to redefine their cultural identities in a new context, and eventually succeeded. Mark and Mary illustrate and confirm Ogbu's cultural model theory.

Vince and Lynn, however, do not really demonstrate or validate Ogbu's idea of "involuntary immigrants," because they achieved a certain level of success despite belonging to a minority group. Of the two, Lynn developed the more oppositional identity, perhaps due to her age and the present social context, which may be less hopeful for minorities.

Jonathan Kozol

In *Savage Inequalities* and particularly in *Amazing Grace*, Kozol takes us on a journey into a world that is closer to Victor Hugo's nineteenth-century France than to a modern, technologically advanced nation in the twenty-first century. Even though he may not even mention the word resilience, his accounts of people affected by poverty and inequality at the bottom of the social ladder, his testimony of children let down by our educational and social system—those who would otherwise be invisible to middle-class America—are right at the core of this study. The seven respondents in this research all illustrate Kozol's message.

DISCUSSION AND IMPLICATIONS

Resilience is a transformational process, not a static and immutable feature of individuals.

The findings of this study suggest, as some have already intimated, that resilience is not an individual feature with which one is simply born, like brown eyes or red hair. Furthermore, in the process showed in table 6-1, resilience does not appear as a special strategy or personal characteristic. Rather, it appears to be part of the whole process described in table 6-1. Without adversity, one cannot show resilience. Similarly, without enabling conditions or coping strategies, resilience does not appear to exist, yet it cannot be identified as one specific category. This study suggests that resilience is part of a transformational process from adversity to achievement.

Measuring resilience is meaningless and pointless.

If resilience is a process rather than a trait, any attempt to measure it in individuals may be futile. Measuring brings with it the notion of comparison, another pointless activity with regard to resilience. One would be very hard-pressed to say who among the seven respondents was the most resilient or the least resilient. It is simply impossible to establish any comparison or ranking among them. Some would argue that the seven respondents showed more resilience than individuals who did not succeed. While the findings of this study do not permit me to answer this argument, I would simply answer that—as a social process rather than a personal measure—whenever resilience is absent, it is our collective social and cultural engagement that is deficient.

Resilience is a process that requires more than just one individual.

The categories that emerged from the data show that resilience was the result of social interaction of individual traits such as perseverance, resistance, and enabling conditions. The latter category shows the importance of social intervention in facilitating resilience among low-income, working-class students.

In addition, the more severe adversity is, the more effects adversity will have on individuals, and the more social intervention will be necessary. It also shows how the dominant culture and social order can aggravate faces of adversity for low-income students. Recent social policy that has stressed the importance of "self-reliance" and the "new social contract," which eliminates safety measures for populations at risk, will only intensify poverty and adversity among people who are already at the bottom of the social ladder.

Resilience helps low-income students bridge the educational gap and cross class boundaries.

Undeniably, resilience as a transformational process helped the seven respondents chart a new course for themselves. With much more effort than their middle-class counterparts, they were able to achieve a significantly high level of success. The persistent achievement gap between social classes can be reduced when individual strategies and enabling social conditions interact. This is cause for hope and concern; the former because it refutes theories of social determinism, the latter because it transfers the burden of responsibility from the individual alone to a shared accountability among individuals, social institutions, and lawmakers.

When lawmakers who, for the most part, come from privileged backgrounds (and are therefore without an intimate understanding of social adversity), make choices guided by a philosophy of individualism and social Darwinism with regard to social programs, health programs, or educational reform, there is indeed cause for concern. Without a growing awareness of the need for shared accountability, the gap between privileged and underprivileged will continue to exist and the tenets of democracy will become more and more fragile.

Social institutions have a role to play and a responsibility in bridging the gap between achievers and nonachievers.

None of the seven respondents succeeded on his or her own. Family, school, church, and community all played a crucial role in enabling or disabling resilience. In the end, the seven respondents prevailed against adversity because at least one of these institutions "stepped in" and played a positive role in their lives. Social institutions are not abstract entities; their fabric is made of us all. It is important to recognize and act upon it. This implies that more individual involvement and even activism for the collective good is needed from us.

Resilience is social as much as psychological or personal.

Findings in this study show that, contrary to what has been said, resilience does not only belong to the realm of psychology but also to the public arena. Psychology provides good explanations of individual disorders or pathology, but poverty is not pathological. Poverty belongs to the social arena where the public lives. This simple fact represents a much-needed cultural paradigm shift in American society. Somehow, privileged and underprivileged individuals alike have come to believe that their social status is a reflection of their individual merit, regardless of circumstances. Even Lynn and Mark, who had overcome remarkable odds against them, adhered to that belief. They both felt that failure in school is the result of a wish to fail. This belief is deeply ingrained in our culture, where we believe that individual responsibility is paramount. Other cultures view this issue differently and may very well provide a better balance in the individual versus collective responsibility debate.

Policy makers can make or break resilience.

Imagine for a moment that instead of passing the Civil Rights Act in 1964, a majority of lawmakers at that time would have voted against it. This decision would have dramatically affected Vince and millions of other African Americans waiting for an opportunity to receive an education and cross class boundaries. Vince would not have been admitted to the University of Chicago, may not have struggled and prevailed to obtain his master's degree, and would probably not hold his current position as executive.

When lawmakers vote to cut funds for underprivileged students, they are perpetuating a cycle of inequalities in our society. Often, it is difficult to see the connections between a vote in Congress that is being discussed in the media for a few days and those affected by those policies, but through the testimonies of real people, the lives of those who are invisible to policy makers and lawmakers become reality.

RECOMMENDATIONS FOR SOCIAL CHANGE

Because all seven respondents had overcome adversity, understandably, they looked back on it with few regrets, although they did admit to being marked by it for life. One can only imagine, then, how adversity may affect those who do not overcome it. How many were lost at the bottom of the social ladder? What can be done to prevent their large numbers from growing? What can be done to reduce their numbers?

This study showed that the answer is not, as some have intimated, only in the individuals themselves, but in a common social effort that includes individuals, schools, families, and social services.

The following list summarizes recommendations stemming from this study for policy makers and educators. Families can help by supporting and modeling these recommendations.

Raise Expectations

Far from penalizing working-class students, raising expectations sends the message that achievement is not beyond their reach. Consider Renée, whose college teacher refused to give her extra credits to compensate for a D grade, and helped her realize that her working habits had to change in order for her to earn her degree. By refusing to "deal" with her, he raised his expectations of her.

End or Curb Labeling

Labeling has a stigmatizing effect that can only impede efforts to surmount one's difficulties. Even though Ray may have actually been mentally retarded, what helped him was a context in which his label did not matter so much and he could be another Ray, someone who could learn, teach, and educate others.

Protect and Challenge

This double recommendation may sound paradoxical, but is not. Remember Lori who started crying in front of a blank map of the United States.

Her teacher consoled her, told her she believed Lori could do it, and challenged her to complete the assignment. Both strategies were necessary to benefit Lori.

Provide Opportunities

None of the respondents would have prevailed against adversity had they not been given opportunities. Opportunities are invitations to cross boundaries and go beyond what is known and familiar. Vince's words, "I have never felt that I was owed anything but a chance," capture this idea.

Improve Social Services

Forty years ago, Lori and her family did not have any health coverage. Her near-blindness was not detected until she started school. Today, eleven million children in America are uninsured; seven in ten Americans losing health insurance are children. It is now an accepted fact that children with untreated illnesses are less able to learn (Children's Defense Fund, 1997). These facts call for more preventive programs in the areas of health, housing, and education.

Foster Culture of Equality

This may be the most challenging recommendation, because it goes against the grain of our culture. It is very difficult to act upon beliefs that are buried in the collective consciousness of a people and not even recognized, yet it is necessary to identify cultural beliefs that perpetuate social injustice. Racial, gender, and social inequalities are deep-rooted products of culture, but cultural beliefs can and do change, however slowly. Forty years after Vince was allowed to attend a racially mixed university, Lynn still feels the effects of racial inequality. Yet in her ongoing fight against it lies the motor of democracy. It is the role of educators and lawmakers to help her and others like her in their struggles.

LOOKING TOWARD THE FUTURE

Despite recommendations and goodwill, a disturbing question remains: When success and failure are built into the system and largely taken for granted, how is it possible to reverse the stigmatizing and long-lasting effects of lower socioeconomic status on educational achievement? It is difficult to even imagine an answer to that question.

Recently, public television featured a documentary on the lives of Susan B. Anthony and Elizabeth Cady Stanton and their struggle for women's rights in the second half of the nineteenth century. These two women leaders worked incessantly for half a century to change the mind-set of a society that considered the very idea of women's right to vote a heresy. In their struggle, they were confronted with many defeats, including conflict with old allies and each other over political strategy. Ultimately, they died without seeing the fruits of their work. Today, women's right to vote is considered a fundamental civil right in our country. However, for these two women, the uncertain outcomes of their struggle must have been overwhelming and, at times, discouraging.

I believe there is a parallel to be drawn between the ongoing struggle for women's rights and the struggle for achievement of poor, working-class youth in American society. We may not see or even imagine a society in which school failure does not correlate with lower socioeconomic status, but a challenge to this cultural orthodoxy is essential—even though we may never see the results of our struggle in our lifetime.

References

Anderson, E. 1990. *Streetwise, Race, Class, and Change in an Urban Community.* Chicago: University of Chicago Press.

Bell, D. 1992. *Faces at the Bottom of the Well: The Permanence of Racism.* New York: Basic.

Bempechat, J. 1998. *Against the Odds: How "At-Risk" Students Exceed Expectations.* San Francisco: Jossey-Bass.

Benard, B. 1996. "Fostering Resiliency in Urban Schools." In *Closing the Achievement Gap: A Vision for Changing Beliefs and Practices,* edited by B. Williams, 96–119. Alexandria, Va.: Association for Supervision and Curriculum Development.

Benard, B. 1996. "Join Us in a National Promotion of Resiliency." *Resiliency in Action* 1:4.

Bond, G. 1980. "Social Economic Status and Educational Achievement." *Anthropology and Education Quarterly* 12: 227–257.

Bourdieu, P., and J. Passeron. 1977. *Reproduction in Education.* Beverly Hills, Calif.: Sage.

Bredo, Eric. 1997. "The Social Construction of Learning." In *Handbook of Academic Learning, Construction of Knowledge,* edited by G. D. Phye. San Diego: Academic.

Bredo, Eric. 1995. "The Emperor Really Has No Clothes: Comments on the Conception of Intelligence." In *The Bell Curve,* a newsletter of the Northern Virginia Social Foundations of Education Program, Spring: 1–3.

Bredo, E., and A. S. Qadir. 1995. "*The Social Implications of Differing Conceptions of Intelligence,*" presented at the American Educational Studies Association conference, Cleveland, Ohio, November 1–5.

Crane, J. 1991. "Effects of Neighborhoods on Dropping out of School and Teenage Childbearing." In *The Urban Underclass,* edited by C. Jenks and P. Peterson, 299–320. Washington, D.C.: Brookings.

Corcoran, M. 1995. "Rags to Rags: Poverty and Mobility in the United States." *Annual Review of Sociology* 21.

Fine, M. 1991. *Framing Dropouts, Notes on the Politics of an Urban Public High School.* Albany: SUNY Press.

Floyd, C. 1996. "Achieving Despite the Odds: A Study of Resilience among a Group of African American High School Seniors." *Journal of Negro Education* 65.

Frankl, V. E. 1984. *Man's Search for Meaning: An Introduction to Logotherapy.* New York: Simon & Schuster.

Freire, P. 1990. *Pedagogy of the Oppressed.* New York: Continuum.

Gibson, M. A. 1988. *Accommodation without Assimilation.* Ithaca, N.Y.: Cornell University Press.

Giroux, H. 1983. *Theory and Resistance in Education.* New York: Bergin and Garvey.

Gould, S. J. 1981. *The Mismeasure of Man.* New York: Norton.

Henderson, N. 1996. "The Faces of Resiliency." *Resiliency in Action* 1:12–15.

Herrnstein, R. J., and C. Murray. 1994. *The Bell Curve: The Reshaping of American Life by Difference in Intelligence.* New York: Free Press.

Hirsch, Jr., E. D. 1996. *The Schools We Need and Why We Don't Have Them.* New York: Doubleday.

Jankowski, M. S. 1991. *Islands in the Street, Gangs and American Urban Society.* Berkeley: University of California Press.

Katz, M., ed. 1993. *The "Underclass" Debate: Lessons from History.* Princeton, N.J.: Princeton University Press.

Kozol, J. 1995. *Amazing Grace.* New York: Crown.

Kozol, J. 1991. *Savage Inequalities.* New York: Harper Perennials.

Luttwak, E. N. 1996. "America Is Becoming a Third World Country." In *America Beyond 2001: Opposing Viewpoints,* 240–246. San Diego, Calif.: Greenhaven Press.

Marks-Greenfield, P., C. Raeff, and B. Quiroz. 1996. "Cultural Values in Learning and Education." In *Closing the Achievement Gap: A Vision for Changing Beliefs and Practices,* edited by B. Williams, 37–55. Alexandria, Va.: Association for Supervision and Curriculum Development.

MacLeod, J. 1987. *Ain't No Making It: Leveled Aspirations in a Low-Income Neighborhood.* Boulder, Colo.: Westview Press.

McDermott, R. P. 1987. "Achieving School Failure." In *Education and Cultural Process,* edited by G. D. Spindler, 82–118. Prospect Heights: Waveland Press.

McDermott, R. P. 1993. "The Acquisition of a Child by a Learning Disability." In *Understanding Practice: Perspectives on Activity and Context,* edited by S. Chaiklin and J. Lave, 269–305. New York: Cambridge University Press.

McDermott, R. P. and H. Varenne. 1995. "Culture as Disability." *Anthropology of Education Quarterly* 26: 324–348.

McDermott, R. P., and H. Varenne, H. 1998. *Successful Failure, The School America Builds.* Boulder, Colo.: Westview Press.

McQuillan, P. J. 1998. *Educational Opportunity in an Urban American High School: A Cultural Analysis*. Albany: SUNY Press.

Mish, Frederick C., ed. 1997. *Merriam–Webster's Collegiate Dictionary, Tenth Edition*. Springfield, Mass.: Merriam–Webster, Inc.

Morrison, T. 1998. *Beloved*. New York: Penguin.

Ogbu, J. U. 1986. "The Consequences of the American Caste System." In *School Achievement of Minority Children: New Perspectives*, edited by U. Neisser, 19–56. Hillsdale, N.J.: Lawrence Erlbaum.

Rodriguez, R. 1982. *Hunger of Memory: The Education of Richard Rodriguez*. New York: Bantam.

Strauss, A., and J. Corbin. 1990. *Basics of Qualitative Research, Grounded Theory: Procedures and Techniques*. Newbury Park, Calif.: Sage Publications, 1–92.

Wang, M. C., and E. W. Gordon, eds. 1994. *Educational Resilience in Inner-City America: Challenges and Prospects*. Hillsdale, N.J.: Lawrence Erlbaum.

Wang, M. C., and J. A. Kovach. 1996. "Bridging the Achievement Gap in Urban Schools: Reducing Educational Segregation and Advancing Resilience-Promoting Strategies." In *Closing the Achievement Gap: A Vision for Changing Beliefs and Practices*, edited by B. Williams, 10–36. Alexandria, Va.: Association for Supervision and Curriculum Development.

Werner, E., and R. Smith. 1996. "How Children Become Resilient: Observations and Cautions." *Resiliency in Action* Winter: 18–28.

West, C. 1994. *Race Matters*. New York: Vintage.

West, N. 1987. *A Cool Million*. New York: Berkley.

Wexler, P. 1982. "Structure, Text, and Subject." In *Cultural and Economic Reproduction in Education*, edited by M. Apple, 275–303. New York: Routledge.

Williams, B. 1996. "The Nature of the Achievement Gap: The Call for a Vision to Guide Change." In *Closing the Achievement Gap: A Vision for Changing Beliefs and Practices*, edited by B. Williams, 1–9. Alexandria, Va.: Association for Supervision and Curriculum Development.

Williams, B. 1996. "A Social Vision for Urban Education: Focused, Comprehensive, and Integrated Change." In *Closing the Achievement Gap: A Vision for Changing Beliefs and Practices*, edited by B. Williams, 148–160. Alexandria, Va.: Association for Supervision and Curriculum Development.

Wilson, W. J. 1987. *The Truly Disadvantaged: The Inner City, the Underclass, and Public Policy*. Chicago: University of Chicago Press.

About the Author

Born in England and raised in North Africa and France, Rosa Aronson has been living in the United States since 1984. She is an associate director at the National Association of Secondary School Principals' Foundation, the Trust to Reach Education Excellence.